GREEN MOUNTAINS

Green Mountains

Bernard O'Reilly

envirobook

Published by Envirobook, a division of Trekaway Pty. Ltd.
7 Close Street, Canterbury NSW 2193
Telephone: 02 9787 1955   www.envirobook.com.au

First published in 1941–42
Reprinted many times.
This edition printed in 2008

National Library of Australia
Cataloguing-in-Publication data:
O'Reilly, Bernard, 1903-1975.
    Green Mountains.
    ISBN 9780858810587.
    1. O'Reilly, Bernard, 1903-1975. 2. Pioneers -
    Queensland - Lamington National Park - Biography.
    3. Frontier and pioneer life - Queensland - Lamington
    National Park. 4. Aircraft accidents - Queensland. 5.
    Lamington National Park (Qld.) - Social life and customs.
    6. Blue Mountains Region (N.S.W.) - Social life and
    customs. I. Title.
994.3204092

Typeset and designed by Bungoona Technologies Pty. Ltd.
Grays Point NSW 2232, Telephone: 02 9526 6199.
Set in 10/12 Bookman.

Cover photograph: Rod Westacott
Line drawings by James Wieneke

Printed in China by Bookbuilders

Contents

Part One

CHAPTER I

The Search

ON Wednesday, 17th February 1937, day broke sullenly without the usual rich reds and browns which attend a Queensland mountain sunrise.

A pale grey scum had spread itself over the sky from the sea, deepening in colour from the distant coastline; an occasional puff of cool wind from the south-east combined with the ominous sky in heralding one of the most violent cyclones which ever swept our mountain top. All through the day the peculiar scum of unbroken cloud gradually deepened in colour from pale grey to dull leaden, and the breeze, though somewhat erratic, steadily freshened.

Next morning, I awoke with the jungle roaring like an angry sea. Stinging, hard-driven rain bit my face like sleet, and low, wind-blown clouds tore through the jungle trees and over the ridge tops like white racehorses. It was a wild, windswept, boisterous day, but not unpleasant to mountain dwellers, who are accustomed to having their weather served up on the same rugged, lavish scale as their scenery. I took advantage of the rain that day to plant clover and couch grass seed in a new clearing, and at dark we settled down to another wild night.

Before dawn on Friday, I awoke to find my little house shivering from the hammer blows of a raging cyclone, and at dawn I went out to find the air full of flying leaves, and with every gust, a crash from the jungle told of the destruction being wrought. Progress down the paddocks was slow; it meant crouching behind a stump until a lull came, and then sprinting for the next cover. The cows were huddled in sheltered windbreaks, and nothing on earth would induce them to leave, so we left them there for the whole day without being milked.

A conservative estimate of the wind velocity over the McPhersons all that day would be eighty miles per hour – many a lesser wind has wrecked a town. Naturally, no aeroplane would have taken off under such conditions, and I have since learned that the ferocity of the hurricane was confined to the upper air, and the wind at Archerfield Aerodrome, Brisbane, was not abnormal.

I spent the morning attending to the stock. The poddy calves, in particular, were having a very bad time, and temporary shelters were made to keep the terrific wind and driving rain from them. After one o'clock I went up to our tiny dairy cottage, and while it rocked in the wind like a ship at sea, I cooked my lunch, every gust blowing the smoke back down the chimney.

While thus engaged, I had no means of knowing that over twenty miles away to the west, across great jungle clad ranges and gorges, three men were struggling from the wreck of a stricken airliner.

The late afternoon showed a definite lessening of the rain and by eight o'clock the wind had begun to drop. Next morning calm reigned; the trees in the open were mostly stripped of their leaves and many of their branches, and had a peculiar old-world wintry look. The atmosphere was cleaned of dust, smoke and haze, and the visibility that morning was clearer than I can ever remember it to be.

Buildings were clearly visible in Brisbane, seventy miles north. The Glasshouse Mountains, over one hundred miles, and the Blackall Range, one hundred and thirty miles away, stood out clearcut and blue against the northern sky.

Down in the troughs between the great billowing ranges of evergreen jungle, torrents revived by the rains roared their way towards the lowlands. The warming sun coaxed little plumes of mist from the drenched landscape, but the sparkling morning gave me no clue to the terrible secret hidden in the heart of the grim McPhersons.

Four miles of our telephone line lay on the ground, so an early start was made that morning to pick up and join this. Masses of leaves which had been stripped from the trees lay in some places knee-deep on the track, and at every few yards large limbs blocked the way. Huge trees, crashed and split in an incredible way, lay along the track, and vivid in my memory is the spot where the top of a glorious Wheel of Fire tree in full bloom had smashed into the middle of the road, scattering its blood-red blossoms with a reckless hand.

From my cousin's house at ten o'clock that morning came my first news of the missing airliner. He had received it over the radio, with the further information that it had last been seen south of Coff's Harbour.

Our anxiety concerning it grew as the days went on; it was an almost personal anxiety. Those splendid machines flew over our house twice daily. They were links with civilisation, and we looked forward eagerly to their comings and goings. We even set our clocks by them.

For the week that followed, there was enacted the most intensive aerial search in Australian history. Australia's Air Force and nearly every civil aeroplane on the east coast joined in combing the whole route. Exact figures are not available but it is well known that many thousands of pounds were expended on the search. Since then recent history has shown that the U.S.A. Government spent five million dollars on the fruitless search for Amelia Earheart.

Finally it was decided to abandon the search. Mrs. Proud – mother of one of the missing passengers – then offered five hundred pounds towards the continuance of the aerial search which had proved fruitless. The offer was not taken up by either the Air Force or the civil authorities.

Anxiously we stood by the radio during news sessions hoping for word. Little hope was left to us when we heard that the liner was missing over the wild Hawkesbury country near Sydney, and then, when the wreckage was "seen" out to sea off Palm Beach, we regretfully said goodbye to Captain Boyden and his gallant company, and considered the sad chapter closed.

By the time a week had gone by, it had been established beyond all doubt that the Stinson had been lost south of the Hawkesbury. Not only had it been "seen" and "heard" by casual observers, but its appearance had actually been recorded in the log of a steamer off Barrenjoey Heads. In the minds of the public, of whom I was one, there could be but one answer to the riddle – the ocean. Even the people who lived at the head of Widgee Creek and who had seen the plane go into a cloud bank, perhaps a bare four minutes before it crashed, were forced to believe the overwhelming weight of evidence supplied by press and radio.

This being the case, why in the name of all that is sane and reasonable, should a man go out to search nearly four hundred miles away from where the plane was last seen; that is what has puzzled most of the people whom I have met, and that, too, has given rise to the frequent question, "Was it a hunch or was it reasoning?" The answer must be, "It was not a hunch, nor do I believe that such a thing as a hunch exists." In ascribing my action to reasoning, I am not ruling out the possibility of Divine intervention. To me it seems that if God wished to intervene and save two men beyond ordinary aid, He would not necessarily do so miraculously, nor would He inspire anyone with a blind unreasoning impulse to go and do His will, but it seems quite natural that He would inspire in a man the reasoning and initiative which would send that man out on his own accord; the fact that the man so chosen had spent most of his life in unwittingly fitting himself out for just such a job seems to further indicate a clear purpose behind it all – that of course, is the way it appears to me.

We now come to Friday, the eighth day after the crash, and the day in which my Great Idea was born. It was on Friday morning, exactly a week after the crash, and the day before I set out on my search, that Viola and I went down to Kerry to visit my brother Herb at his little farm. He had a nice batch of cows and lots of pigs – spotted little fellows which look like tiger cats. It was rather a hot day and I spent it going round with him, helping to water the stock and cutting feed for the cows and pigs.

In the morning, while we worked, Herb and I talked quite a lot about the Stinson. He had seen it go over on the previous Friday, flying into the wind towards the cloudbank McPhersons, holding its ordinary course towards Lismore. Later, we went over to his house for lunch. It was a small house, nice and new, smelling of fresh pine resin and new paint. While I was waiting for lunch I dug into a few old newspapers. Thanks to the break in our communications through the cyclone, and the flood to follow, I had scarcely seen a newspaper during the week. They were full of theories and counter-theories concerning the missing airliner, and one prominent paper published two days after the plane was reported missing, assured us, in type which extended across the front page, that the machine had got to within fifteen minutes of its destination in Sydney. In a maze of contradictory evidence and theories advanced by six different papers, I gleaned one definite fact, and that fact was to send me out on my search.

It was the definite report that on the afternoon of Friday the nineteenth, people had waited in vain at Lismore for the arrival of the airliner. Explanation of the plane's omission to call at Lismore was that it had gone directly down the coast from Brisbane to avoid the bad weather over the mountains; but by this time, I was in possession of the fact that the plane had not gone down the coast. Hundreds of people in my district had seen it disappear into the ranges towards Lismore; people waited in vain for its arrival in Lismore. What was the answer? It dawned upon me that the answer was lying somewhere up in the jungle and gorges of the McPherson Range.

That night, I could not get home quickly enough.

Darkness overtook us as we rode towards home up the mountainside. Mopokes called from across the gorge; here and there a dingo sent his protest to high heaven; but I was busy turning over plans for my search, and working out the programme. Near home, the moon came up and sprinkled the jungle with silver.

We got to the home gate, and Rhelma's blue cattle pup, Kettelorg, barked at us. No doubt he thought we had no right to come home so late.

By this time my plan was definitely formed. Including the area over the New South Wales border, there are roughly eighty thousand acres of unbroken, trackless jungle on the McPherson Ranges, in most of which visibility is limited to ten yards; to suggest that one man could thoroughly search such an area is too absurd for words. Three life times would be all too short for such a job. There must be a plan of action. Next morning I telephoned my friend, Bob Stephens, at the head of the Albert River. He and his immediate neighbours were, as far as I understood, the last people to see the plane in flight, and from him I got a final checkup on the position and its approximate course. We had in our house a copy of the latest Aerial Survey Map of the McPhersons. This map was reconstructed from aerial photographs taken at an altitude of fourteen thousand feet, and though lacking in minor detail, it is the best available guide to the topography of the range.

On this map, with an ordinary foot rule and pencil, I drew a straight line from the point where the airliner was last seen, along the line of flight towards Lismore, as I believed it to be. This plotted line contacted four high mountain ranges, and I reasoned that, if the missing liner was to be found in this locality, it would necessarily be on the northern slopes of any of these four.

Such was the plan of action; it looks very plain and ordinary now, but it had one great advantage – it worked. Other preparations for the journey were simple: a wire handle was put in a two pound jam tin, so that it would serve the double purpose of a Billy can and drinking cup; two loaves of bread, a pound of butter and half a dozen onions, and finally tea and sugar, went into the little tucker bag. Mother, now seventy-five years old, seemed proud of the fact that I alone of the Queensland people was setting out to search, but there was a lot of uneasiness too which she tried hard to conceal. One of my feet was inflamed from where a rusty nail had pierced it two days before. I opened this up and was pouring iodine into it, when Rhelma (now four years) found me. She said: "Daddy, that stuff will sting you," but I had already found that out. Then, "Daddy, where are you going?" She was told, and then there was the inevitable, "Daddy, can I go too?" Reasons were advanced against this. "Well, will you bring the aeroplane home with you?" This was more in the nature of a demand, than as an alternative.

Viola came in then and said, "I wish I could go with you," and the Littlefeller said, "Mummy, I want to go too," with renewed hope. Viola made me take some snakebite antidote (permanganate crystals) and a safety-razor blade. Mother gave me a long piece of cord to serve as a ligature (or for spare boot laces!) Whenever we need a piece of string in our family, we naturally go to Mother for it. She collects it painstakingly from every parcel which arrives at the homestead and methodically places it in her string bag.

From our house there is a riding track to Mount Bethongabel – a glorious lookout point on the border of New South Wales about four thousand feet above sea level. To this point I had planned to ride; so an old chestnut mare called The Great Unknown (Heaven only knows why!) was quickly saddled. She is a poor hack, as our horses go, but was the only one in the house paddock at the time. And so, with a quick, "Expect me when you see me," we went dashing off along the border track.

Arriving at Bethongabel, I tied Great Unknown's rein to the stirrup, pointed her towards home, and said "Shoo!" She thought this was too good to be true and was looking around for the catch, but when she found that it was fair dinkum she set off like a Melbourne Cup Winner – just in case I should change my mind. From here it was my plan to follow the backbone of the McPhersons west to the first of the four high lateral spurs, where I reasoned that the unfortunate liner may have crashed. For another two miles I was assisted by the track to the Valley of Echoes, another spot of surpassing beauty opened up by my brothers in 1912. From here on it was trackless, lawyer-vine jungle. And what is it like? Imagine trees growing so closely together that their tops interlace in one continuous canopy; imagine that canopy so enveloped and smothered with leafy vine that it would be actually possible to travel for miles on the treetops without coming to earth; so dense that it lets in only an occasional chink of sunlight on a bright day; dripping with moisture from the eternally brooding clouds.

And what of the floor of this jungle? Visibility is limited to ten yards by a tangle of tough green vine as dense as wire netting, and covered with murderous thorns. Great logs left by cyclones lie in the way, but do not stand on one. You will go knee deep into a wet pulpy morass, which is half fungus. Travelling in the jungle on a cloudy day is like travelling in a dense fog, and you can navigate by reckoning only. You can see by the map that there are so many ridges and so many gorges between you and a given spot, so you check them off as you go. "And how do you keep a straight course?" perhaps you are asking. Well, no course in this country can be exactly straight; you tack about to find the easiest way down the cliffs and the easiest grade up the other side of the gorge, but you know by your map that the big lateral ranges are running from south to north, and if you cut them at right angles, you must be going west. Then, too, the jungle is full of other signs to tell you the points of the compass. Northern and eastern slopes are always matted with the heaviest growths of lawyer and raspberry-vine, while southern slopes give way to forests of fern- trees and great clusters of lilies. Also, the southern side of a tree is heavily covered with lichen and moss, while the northern side shows a smooth bole. It is a great help to have a knowledge of trees and shrubs which bloom in this area. Down in the lower jungles at the foot of the ranges, a certain species of tree will bloom six weeks earlier than the same species on the loftiest heights. At the lower levels, the tree will be going to seed, while at two thousand feet it will be blooming, at four thousand feet it will be in early bud. So with a good local knowledge of plants, it is possible to estimate your altitude very accurately, and since altitudes are marked on the map this is a very important thing. The same sliding scale applies to the nesting of birds, so that all nature is willing and anxious to help, if you will only take the trouble to notice. The prevailing winds in the McPhersons are from the south, and all trees in exposed places have a heavy lean to the north.

Late that afternoon I located a camp site which marked the farthest point of a previous exploration. That was in 1918, when Herb and I had gone to accompany the late Archibald Meston on a trip to Lamington Plateau by way of the border ranges. We had battled through the lawyer-vine all that day and started for home next morning without having covered a third of the distance. The camp of that night so long ago was still a vivid memory. A high wind roared in the jungle blowing our smoky fire with a snowstorm of ashes, alternately towards and away from us.

Archibald Meston, affectionately known as the Father of Queensland, was a most picturesque figure. He was a journalist, historian, explorer and probably the greatest authority on Australian aboriginals and native dialects. I shall always remember his keen old face and piercing eyes in the leaping firelight, as he told his eerie tales of early Queensland, while the ashes blew into his white hair and the jungle roared its grand organ solo overhead.

About two o'clock in the morning, when Herb got up to rebuild the fire, a great yellow dingo was standing in the glow of the dying embers. All these scenes came back very vividly to me as I stood looking at a charred log, which had survived the nineteen intervening years.'

About sunset I was dipping down to the head of a gorge where water would be found for the evening billy. A tawny mass disentangled itself from the jungle floor ahead. It was a spotted tiger cat, one of the rarest and most ferocious of Australian animals. He had been eating a freshly killed ringtailed possum. The tiger, which is now one of the rarest of Australian animals, and one of the most ferocious, climbed a small sapling to head height, and regarded his first human visitor with a fearless and unfriendly eye. The tiger cat while being one of the rarest of Australian animals is nevertheless plentiful in these parts. The green twilight of the timber had deepened into blackness by the time water was found, and then from the moss banks and damp hillsides around the water there shone out thousands of points of green light, which were glow-worms and luminous fungi.

If you have ever looked down on Sydney at night from Lapstone Hill, or on Brisbane from Mount Cootha, and could you imagine these lights turned to pale green, then you will have some idea of the illuminations of the fairy city which flanked my camp on the first night of the Stinson search.

The little glow-worms are worthy of mention. They shine their green headlights on a sticky web so that tiny insects, attracted by the light, are easily trapped. There are many forms of luminous fungi. The largest is a fan-shaped variety, which grows tier upon tier on rotting tree trunk like a phosphorescent staircase. A newspaper can easily be read by their light. Then we have a tiny toadstool kind, its little umbrella smaller than a threepenny piece, and showing quite a brilliant green light.

There is also a luminous thread fungus, which eats its way through fallen logs, leaves and twigs on the ground, and gives patches of brilliance like scattered nebulae from the Milky Way. At the height of the rainy season, the whole jungle floor may be lit with this irregular light. On thundery summer nights myriads of twinkling fireflies add a final touch to this fairyland.

With wet wood, damp ground and no blanket, sleep was just about impossible, but Nature spread itself to keep me entertained. First, some black phalangers fought and screamed horribly in the vines overhead. I suppose they only lost some fur, but it sounded as though there would not be an animal left alive by morning. Later, as the moon struggled out of a cloud mass, a large pack of dingoes commenced to howl away down the gorge. The tones of their howlings were spread over an octave, and I thought of a chorus of banshees. I thought, too, that dingoes howl in packs about dead bodies, and a nasty cold feeling got hold of me. Down in that gorge, there might have been what?

The wind freshened during the night, and misty rain fell at intervals. Just before dawn, a light doze was broken by the unearthly screams of a powerful owl in the trees overhead. Few Australians know much about this bird. He is as large and strong as our great wedge-tailed eagle. Mr. S.W. Jackson once told me that powerful owls were known to tear fully grown koalas to pieces. It is a great pity for Nature lovers that a large part of the jungle wild life is nocturnal.

A tiny night rambler in our timber is the dormouse possum, the smallest of our marsupials, about the size of a fully grown mouse; he sleeps through the winter in a nest deep in a hollow tree. To my sister, Molly, fell the honour of first locating this little fellow in southern Queensland. She found one in daylight in the big timber a hundred yards from our house. The little animal was paralysed. We tried to restore, it with food, but it died. Its body was received with much joy by Mr. Heber Longman, Director of the Brisbane Museum. A subsequent press notice brought an unexpected sequel; a self-righteous busybody in Brisbane wrote to my sister, reprimanding her for "slaying a beautiful wild creature". Such was her reward for trying to save the life of a little animal. It was ironical that such a letter should have been written to a member of a family which for a generation was the sole guardian of a wild life sanctuary.

Breakfast before dawn, and my last onion but one (should have brought more – roast onion is good). Half an hour from camp brought me to one of the most glorious cascades I have ever seen, as high and as beautiful as our own lovely Elabana, back near home. I thought that if my madcap search did nothing else, it would be well worthwhile in the discovery of this fall.

Climbing out of the gorge from my waterfall tension increased, for I was climbing the first of the four lateral ranges, on any one of which I reasoned that the wreck might be.

By eight o'clock I was on the summit of its southern extremity, Mt. Throakban, enveloped in white clouds. None of us had ever been to Mt. Throakban, though its great green cone away to the south-east had beckoned enticingly to young explorers. It was not a dangerous undertaking, but it would have entailed a lot of hard work and time and there were many nearer gorges and peaks which would more richly reward exploration. The peak and its surrounding country are smothered in tangled growth of equatorial luxuriance and never a day of the three hundred and sixty-five passed without cloud on its summit. Throakban might well have been named The Cloudmaker. It is the favourite breeding ground of the brief and violent local storms which are a feature of the McPhersons in summer.

Here I was on Throakban at last, waiting for the cloud to lift sufficiently to permit me a view. For fifteen minutes I stood in cool moist wind, looking into a grey blank, and then suddenly the racing clouds split, and a vast green sea of ranges and gorges came into view to the west. It gave a good view of the three remaining ranges in the plotted line of flight. Here and there were creamy white splashes which I knew to be trees in bloom, and then suddenly I saw something which made me jump. Eight miles away by the map, on the third range, Lamington Plateau, just where it swelled up to join the border range, was a treetop which was light brown. In Spring, when trees are getting fresh leaf growths, it is not uncommon to see a brownish treetop, but this was late summer. The tree must have been dying; what had caused that? Natural causes? No; trees dying that way die a branch at a time. Lightning perhaps? But why in all that ocean of trees was this one freshly killed tree situated where the straight pencil-line crossed my map? Fire? No natural fire had occurred in that dripping rain forest since the world began. But a hundred gallons of petrol. Swiftly the clammy clouds swooped down again; I put down my head and tore into the soaking green jungle, in my haste to traverse the gorges and jungled ranges which lay between me and that clue. The going was all blind; I did not see that tree again until I was twenty yards from it eight hours later.

Every here and there was evidence of cyclone violence – trees that had split as they smashed off, leaving huge, jagged, yellow splinters pointing upwards. Other trees had been uprooted, their great buttresses lifting a mound of red earth twelve feet high. At one place the ground was paved with Pithecolobium flowers. These have a brush flower of creamy white, and tips of the brush appear as though they have been dipped in bright pink. On the morning after the cyclone had abated, little Rhelma found some which had been blown from the trees and she called them Fairy Paintbrushes. That night, after she had gone to sleep, I put her pretty ideas together and made them rhyme. The result is a verse, which may be found in the latter part of this book. It is included in the hope that other little children may like it.

Hours of climbing and descending went by. At one point, on the edge of a two thousand foot cliff, I looked out across the Northern Rivers of New South Wales, spread like a green map and dotted with farmhouses which looked like mushrooms. Just a brief glance, and then I was scrambling down the next gorge.

CHAPTER II

The Discovery

IT must have been pretty well noon, possibly a little bit either way, when the bottom of the gorge was reached, and hunger had been very evident for some hours. Lunch is often delayed by the uncertainty of water – well, here was water, tons of it; or should one say, gallons of it – pouring over an outcrop of brown volcanic rock. Masses of treeferns were gathered round; great lilies were banked on either side; ropes of lawyer-vine, with their palmlike leaves dipped in low festoons over this small torrent; on either side, and meeting overhead, were the ancient Antarctic beeches covered with moss, which dripped from the drifting spray of the waterfalls and from the ever-present moisture which goes with mountains almost eternally enveloped in cloud. All this scene I saw out of one eye; the other just saw the water, and its possibilities for the brewing of tea and having that meal, which was a couple of hours overdue.

Beech twigs sheltered by a great leaning tree were sufficiently dry to start a fire. It was as smoky as "Billyo," but that sort of smoke adds to the tea a flavour which cannot be bought. While the Billy was coming to the boil, the last of the onions went into the fire to roast, and a couple more rounds of toast were made. The quality of this toast cannot be recommended. A fire which consists of fifty per cent smoke, forty-nine per cent blaze and one per cent red coals is not conducive to giving to toast the quality of the product which emerges from your electric toaster. There was still plenty of butter and the sugar was lasting well, so that, apart from the glorious waterfall which I had found that morning, that meal was the one bright patch. Packing up to go on was not a difficult matter this time. Half a loaf of bread was the largest item to go back into the little tucker bag.

Progress up the next range was very slow, for you cannot travel quickly when you have eaten comfortably, especially when the meal has been topped off with lots of black tea. At this stage, too, weariness was beginning to overtake me. The trip had not been just a matter of walking and scrambling over rough country, it had been a battle as tiring as if I had been forcing my way knee deep through rough surf. The morale effect too was depressing, as more and more the seeming hopelessness of my task became apparent to me. The cheerlessness of the dripping underbrush, the grey swirl of the clouds through the timber, the silence of the birds and the lack of human company, all combined to bring my spirits to the lowest ebb as I climbed that first range after lunch.

It was about one o'clock when the top of the range was reached. A close check was kept on these ranges, so that my approximate position on the map could be estimated. Some time was wasted looking for a break in the trees which might permit a glimpse towards Lamington Plateau. I climbed a tree, but its top was in the clouds and a view was impossible. What should I do now? The answer was startling. From the direction of Lamington Plateau – about three miles away by the map – came a short, clear human call, and then another. A human voice in that green wilderness – what could it mean? My first thought was that the call came from where my pencil line crossed the map – from where that dead tree was. Were they the men of the missing plane? Reason ruled this out. Even in the days of the Spartans, human endurance could not have gone so far. No, the calls obviously came from some searcher – someone as foolish as myself, looking in that vast area for a wreck which evidence had shown to be in the sea near Sydney. There was a strong temptation to answer that call, but an answer could only lead to confusion and misunderstanding, and might lead that man miles out of his way on a false trail; my decision was to hold my tongue until I reached Lamington Plateau. Then I would try to contact that mystery voice.

It was only about three miles to the top of Lamington Plateau, but there were a range and two gorges in between. One range is the same as another, and one gorge the same as another. Three hours later, about four o'clock, I stood on the lip of what I believed to be Lamington Plateau. If I had held a straight course, my position would now be near that dead tree, seen eight hours earlier; but there had been no sun and no visibility, so perhaps my reckoning was all wrong. This, too, was the location of those calls. Well, that could easily be tested. Just a matter of waiting until my breath came back for one big "coo-ee". It echoed sharply from across the gorge, a pause then came the mystery call, but this time, so clear and close, that it had the effect of a physical shock. It could not have been more than two hundred yards down through the timber to the left. I answered sharply, and started down in that direction. A second voice joined the first. We exchanged calls to guide me through the thickly meshed tangle.

"Who are they?" "Members of a search party from Lamington district," said Reason. "Survivors of the wrecked plane," said a little voice. "There couldn't be survivors from a crash in this country – not after this time," said Reason. "Why are they on that line on my map where the dead tree was?" said the little voice.

But I put the little voice aside, and refused to become excited. They would be bush chaps, searching like myself. Well, a bit of company would be good after these two lonely days. Perhaps, too, they would be able to spare me a change of tucker, some meat, maybe. Only twenty yards away now. What was this? A big gap in the treetops just ahead. I tore a piece of vine aside to get a better view, the great tree beside the gap was blackened by fire, right to its branches. God in Heaven! What was this? A numbness shot through my limbs, a sort of coldness that was worse than fear and worse than pain or shock, but was a combination of all three; a feeling that has stayed with me through the crowded months in between, that is with me even as I write. Before I looked down, I knew that I would see a mass of smashed and charred metal. It was more than that; it was a horrible, unclean thing, which held the trapped remains of what once were men – a repulsive thing which I could not go near. The voices came again from below the wreck. Two voices – men alive, but in what condition? I stood for a minute, afraid to go on to them, afraid of what I would see.

Proud, I saw first, his eyes far back in his head like those of a corpse, lying as he had lain for ten days on that wet ground with a broken leg that was green and swelling and maggoty. "My God!" I thought, "You have lain all these days in hell, and now I'm too late to save you." Who can describe the anguish I felt in that swift second. Then I turned to Binstead – he tried to shake hands, a poor hand that was like raw meat. His legs, too, were like that, and the legs of his trousers were worn away in crawling over the rocks to bring water.

There was some talk, lots of talk; but who remembers what was said? The first sane remark I remember was Binstead's, "How about boiling the Billy?" There again we have a little echo of the influence of tea in our national life. It bears out too, the thought that wherever men meet together under big trees, whether it be an occasion of pleasure or of work, or adversity or tragedy, there is always the same reaction to the words, "How about boiling the Billy?"

The fire was hard to make with sodden wood

that was like a sponge; hard, too, with hands that shook. Their story came out a little at a time, and it is pieced together here with some knowledge that has been gained since.

The great airliner, flying blind over ranges completely wrapped in cloud, had been caught in the down-draught of a cyclone of probably one hundred miles per hour, and tossed instantaneously into the mountain. When a crash was inevitable, the pilot, Captain Rex Boyden, a gallant digger "War Bird", banked his plane sharply to starboard.

This swift act in his last split second of life saved the lives of the three men on the port side of the machine. Two big trees were chopped off by the impact, then the machine hit squarely on the great tree which had been my guiding beacon. There is still some metal embedded in the tree sixty feet from the ground. The wreck dropped to earth.

The pilots, Boyden and Shepherd slumped forward in their seats. Death was swift and merciful to them and to the two passengers on the starboard side, Graham and Fountain. The cabin filled with black smoke, and then fuel from the burst tanks turned the wreck into a raging furnace. Proud, the first to recover, smashed a window and dropped through to the ground below. Though his leg had a contused fracture he was able, with a desperate effort, to assist Binstead through the narrow opening. Then Binstead helped the young Englishman, Westray.

Although the whole thing had occupied brief seconds, Westray's hands were badly burned. Binstead and Westray helped Proud to a safe distance from the flames. They congratulated one another on their deliverance, but they were not then to know that they had escaped death, only to face a death that was far more terrible: the torture of starvation, exposure and despair.

The red petrol flames roared high amongst the trees and black smoke mingled with the swirling rain clouds, but the clouds and streaming rain screened the fire which might have served as a distress beacon. The wreck burned fiercely for many hours and provided a measure of warmth through that first long, wet night. "Things might have been a lot worse," thought the lost men. "We might have been in amongst those red embers. The hue and cry would be already going, land parties and search planes would be out tomorrow morning. With a bit of luck we shall be found by midday, or within twenty-four hours at the most."

Well it was for their hopes that they knew nothing of the active imaginations which were already tracing the airliner's journey south, step by step, with irrefutable evidence. Past Coff's Harbour, past Kempsey, past Broken Bay to within ten minutes of Sydney.

In spite of the confidence which the men had in an early rescue, Westray decided next morning to go out and speed up the relief party. To understand his decision it would be necessary to know Jim Westray.

He was a brilliant young Englishman on a business trip to Australia and New Zealand. A member of a prominent Warwickshire county family, he had spent many of his vacations climbing alone in the Highlands of Scotland. Mountains and the outdoors, seemed to have been his main hobby. He was also a cricketer above the average.

This fondness for mountains and his sportsman's love of the sporting risk, helped to make light of his lone venture into a strange and terrible country, so that help might come more swiftly to his companions in misfortune. He went, and after the crash of his body through the vine and underbrush had faded from hearing, an occasional cheery call came back to the men at the plane.

Back at the machine there was work to be done. Proud was settled back near the wreck – the only place on that mountain where a broken leg might be kept straight. His leg was roughly bound, the bone was out through the skin. A piece of broken wing fabric from the plane was bent round the leg to form a rough splint. Proud by this time was feverish, water had to be found and carried to him, but how? Binstead raked in the hot remains of the wreck and found a large metal coffee flask with a loop handle. It seemed to be made to order for carrying water. Water was found about three hundred yards away down the mountain, three hundred yards of almost perpendicular range over rocks and through lawyer-vine. It was a big effort for a city man. Binstead was not young; he was a successful wool broker of Sydney, who had done his travelling by car or aeroplane, and had never been called upon to indulge in any violent primitive exercise. He was soon to show that though the training was lacking, the material was good. That first trip was hard, as were the next two, but the thought of imminent rescue buoyed him up. However, days without food, and damp, cold nights without sleep or shelter or adequate clothing are poor food for optimism. Doubt began to come. Machines crossed over them each way on the daily service between Brisbane and Sydney, but in spite of the fires which Binstead made, the jungle roof hid its secret; blue smoke offers no contrast from the eternal blue of the ranges.

Here, Binstead had to make a fateful decision. It was obvious by this time that something had happened to Westray and that help was not forthcoming.

Through a gap in the trees Binstead had seen many miles below, clearings which meant civilization. Should he try his luck – try where a younger, stronger man had failed? Should he try to get out and save his own life while there was still time, before weakness or starvation made the effort impossible; try to get out and leave Proud helpless and feverish, Proud, to whom water was the breath of life? Never could a man be called upon to make a harder decision. Many a man has had a bronze cross pinned on his breast for some deed in the heat of battle, but to choose in cold blood a course which meant death by starvation and exposure is something different from military courage. Binstead could have made an effort to save his own life; it is not certain that he would have succeeded, but one thing is certain, that if he had gone there would now be one more lonely grave on Lamington Plateau – John Proud's.

More days and nights went by – Binstead was crawling now (his last water journey took five hours). He found some ropes of red berries which he carried back to Proud. The ropes were held in his teeth and his greeting, "Here comes mamma bird," is now a matter of history. The berries are not nourishing, but they keep the mouth from becoming dry. They are the fruit of a little palm, *Bacularia monostachya,* and you will find specimens growing in the Sydney Botanical Gardens.

One remark I shall always remember. As the billy was coming to the boil, Binstead asked: "What day is it?" "Sunday," I answered. He then turned to Proud and said, "You were right after all, old man." Day by day Proud had scratched a diary with a pocket knife on a piece of wing metal, from the plane, calmly setting down a record of what had happened, even after hope had gone.

On Saturday, the day before I reached them, an aeroplane circled above them for some minutes. It was Frank Buchanan, It is with deep regret that I must announce the death of Frank Buchanan in a flying accident while piloting an air liner between Salaman and Wan, New Guinea, during bad weather, in February 1941. A fine pilot and a fine young fellow – a young Beaudesert pilot, and the only other Queenslander with the same idea as myself. He had chartered the plane at his own expense, and if it had been possible to see the wreck from the air he would have found it before I did.

All this time I had been trying to collect my scattered wits and decide on some plan of action. Returning home for help was out of the question, it would be well into the fifth day before I could bring back a doctor, and help from that quarter.

Home was twenty-two miles away across impossible country. I knew that somewhere beneath the great cliffs on the New South Wales side there were settlements (the town of Tyalgum later proved to be only a short distance from the wreck), but the great Border walls had only one point of accessibility in those parts and that was almost impossible to find from the Queensland side. Out of the mountains on the Queensland side the settlements of Hillview, Lamington and Christmas Creek were relatively close; these would be my best mark but a way had to be found out to them, and more important still, a way found back again.

I looked at Proud. To my judgment he seemed already beyond medical help, but if there was a chance for him a doctor would have to be on the spot within twenty-four hours. In my own mind there were serious doubts as to whether he would live so long – that was the factor that contributed to my state of mind, the belief that I had been too late. The thing to do was to get to civilisation by the quickest route. Very easy if you knew the quickest route or any route at all for that matter. The map would have been a great help, if I had known whereabouts on it I was supposed to be, but I could only guess and as in many other situations, guessing could be very expensive.

I made ready for my dash for help. The old maroon wool jacket which Viola had knitted for me the previous winter I gave poor Binstead to help cover his rags. There was a brief glance at my map. If that gorge below was the extreme south branch of Christmas Creek – and this later proved correct – the first clearing would be about nine miles away. It was then half-past four. No chance of getting out of the big timber before dark. I threw down the map. It was of glossed paper, mounted on canvas. That night, Binstead spread it over his shoulders; it gave him some protection from the heavy rain.

My last words were: "I'll bring back a doctor and a hundred men." It was easy to decide upon the direction, simply the shortest cut to the gorge. That way would have been taken anyhow; the Englishman had gone that way, and as it had been a day of miracles, I had hopes of finding him alive also. His tracks deep in the wet leaf mould were easy to follow in country where no white man had ever gone before. The first part of the journey followed Binstead's water track, and there was more than one pathetic reminder of his journeys. Here a large piece of torn clothing, there a shoe which had come off when there was no strength left to put it back on.

CHAPTER III

The Rescue

I followed the Englishman's tracks into difficult and dangerous country, down cliffs of loose rock covered with great Bird's Nest ferns which give a false sense of security, down almost perpendicular slopes of loose earth, studded with treeferns; down until suddenly, through a screen of palm trees I saw the torrent, boiling white around great moss covered boulders. I looked for tracks, but there was no need. The Englishman had gone the right way. Who had taught him the old bushman's trick of following running water when lost? I followed for about a third of a mile. Here progress was blocked by a waterfall which dropped thirty feet. The best way to get around this was to the right. The tracks went to the right, ahead of me. Here he made his fatal mistake. The cliff to the right was completely covered with giant Helmholtzia lilies with sabrelike leaves, seven feet long. These gave apparently safe hand and foothold to the bottom of the cliff. Westray was not to know that there is nothing more brittle or treacherous than those safe-looking footholds. A mass of torn out and broken lilies told their own story. I expected to find him lying on the broken blue rocks at the foot of that drop, but found instead that he had gone on, crawling this time, miles down that torrent bed with its green, slimy boulders, around four more waterfalls. I followed with my heart in my throat – knowing what I would find, and expecting every twist of the gorge to reveal it.

Ah! There was my man just ahead, sitting with his back against a big boulder. "Hullo!" I shouted. "Hoy, there!" He didn't move. Must have been asleep. I came round the front of the rock.

There was no need for a second look. The Englishman was dead. There was a burntout cigarette stump between his fingers. His right shoe and sock were off. He'd been bathing a smashed ankle in the torrent beside him; his face had injuries. He was facing – gazing, it seemed – down the gorge to where lay safety and civilisation, towards which he had unerringly gone from the moment he had left the wreck. Beside him on a smaller rock lay a silver cigarette case – Proud's. I heard later that there had been a sharing up of cigarettes on that Saturday morning. I took a mildewed wallet from his inside breast pocket; my hand was shaking.

Westray was the name on his papers, J.G. Westray. There was currency, too, blue with mould.

That wallet represented enough to keep a family in comfort for more than a year, and it lay in the pocket of a man who had died for want of attention and nourishment.

No time now to give way to the savage hurt which I felt; there were two other men dying for want of attention, and every second was priceless – the light was fading, and if caught in that strange gorge in jungle night that was as black as the pit of Hell, fatal delay might occur. So I ran off, and left Jim Westray. Time will never remove that picture of him, sitting with his back to the rock.

Miles behind him at the wreck lay the two stricken fellow travellers whom he had striven to help, even unto death. Behind him, too, was the cliff where he had fallen, and in between the miles of terrible stream bed and waterfalls over which he had dragged his broken body. A feat of endurance beyond human conception. Around him in the green twilight of the lofty jungle was the unearthly beauty of palm, fern, orchid and vine; beside him tumbled the wild creek and from around a bend the deep musical note of a waterfall dropping into a deep black pool. But he faced, unseeing, down towards the land of people and everyday things, the goal he had tried for: cities, England, Home.

It is given to few men to die so gloriously in the service of others, or to attain such heights of self-sacrifice and manly endurance. All red-blooded men should envy Jim Westray, who sleeps in his orchid covered grave amidst some of the most beautiful scenery in the world – another little spot "Forever England". Westray did not die in vain; a million young Australians will be richer for the example of his sacrifice.

So I ran off and left Westray, his wallet in my pocket burning against my thigh, ran down the treacherous stream bed, falling against rocks, getting up to run on, numb and blinded by shock and emotion, down waterfalls, waist deep through pools. Night closed in. Nothing now to guide me save a grey reflection on the water; was there no end to this? Was I lost? Was this Christmas Creek gorge? Were there cliffs and high waterfalls in front of me? Would someone find me sitting on a boulder, gazing, gazing?

All track of time went, and all feeling from my body. I seemed to be running an obstacle race in the bed of a black underground river, miles down in the earth. One sharp thought only in all the chaos: "Hurry! Proud is dying."

A break in the timber to the left, and the jungle gave way to great white gums, which towered dimly above. I left the water and turned across open flats, which were good travelling; then I struck a broad timber track. Suddenly, close by, the crack of a rifle.

"Hoy!" I yelled with more relief than I've ever felt.

"Hoy!" came back a cheery, youthful voice. "I'm just having a pot at some flying foxes!" and then – "Where the hell did you come from?"

By this time there had come within the light of his hurricane lantern a vision with wet hair in his eyes, torn clothes, dripping with sweat and creek water, with a stubble of whisker and some dried blood to make the scarecrow complete.

"I've found that missing aeroplane," I gasped, "and there are two men still alive."

The news was through. To how many people in

Australia next day did those words bring a thrill. Not of joy or happiness, but of horror. To expect seven dead men so long after the crash was the natural, though terrible thing; but two men, suffering severely from shock and injury, alive on the eleventh day, without food, shelter or medical attention: men who had already been through worse than death – what was their condition now? Could they possibly be saved? How many people will forget the horror of the picture first conjured up by those words – "Two men STILL alive."

Swiftly my questions were answered: he was a Buchanan. Yes, this was Christmas Creek; Lamington was nine miles away; Yes, I could telephone from the house at Lamington, and he would ride down and show me the way.

"There's some tea in the Billy," I was told. "Have some while I run in the horses."

Sitting on an empty kerosene case, swigging tea that was hot and strong and black, I came steadily back to earth – back, too, to the consciousness of a thousand cuts and thorns, bruises and aches; of wet smelly clothes that clung to me – they were to continue to cling for another forty-eight hours.

There must be reserves in all of us which are not apparent until called upon. As I sat on that box I felt myself to be done, it was a case which could only be described as complete exhaustion; there seemed to be no question of carrying on even though my mind refused to quit. But for the thought of what was behind me I'd have sunk to the floor, wet clothing and all, and slept the clock round. I think it was the very agony of the knowledge that those men would be let down after all, which burned through me and gave me the nervous energy to go on, after bodily strength had given out. I rose and carried on for two more nights and days.

The horses were ready. I remember lengthening my stirrups. They had been too short for my long legs. The leathers were stiff and the buckles hard to work; the horse fidgeted and I thought him flighty as we left the friendly lantern for the dark track. I never did like a strange horse at night. Again, time ceased to exist; there were deep creek crossings, with water that came to the saddle flaps, and inky patches of underbrush lit by fireflies. At last the mountains began to fall back and we came on over flats and farming land, and cleared country with great grey gums at intervals along the road, then a house that owned a utility truck. Henry Burgess sized up the situation at once and in as little time it takes to tell, we had paddocked our horses and he was speeding us on.

Lamington at last, and John Buchanan's house with a telephone. John met us on the steps. John, a lean, slow-spoken bushman with greying hair, showed no frenzy of excitement at the news. He is typical of a generation of men who have cut their living from the virgin bush, who have had to depend on their own resources, to overcome each new obstacle as they met it, who had done their own thinking, and have been their own advisers. His questions were practical and the motive behind them constructive, with the one end – to get the live men out as quickly as possible. It was steadying to find a man so strong and calm when my nerve was going. The first thing to do was to ring Airlines of Australia, and from them I received a mandate to organise the rescue as I thought fit, since I was on the spot and knew the conditions.

I was fortunate to have at my elbow the man who knew more of Lamington Plateau than any other. This done, we got Bob Stephens on the telephone. His brothers also plugged in on the party wire, and a hurried conference took place. The plan of action was swiftly decided upon. Five minutes it took, but five years of study could not have revealed a flaw in it, or any means by which the stricken men could have been brought to hospital one minute sooner than they were.

John Buchanan was to take every man that could be mustered up an open forest ridge on to the low end of Lamington Plateau, and at dawn commence cutting the track up the gradually sloping backbone of the range to the wreck. This was the track for the stretchers to be carried over. I was to lead another party, comprising the doctor, the four Stephens brothers, and a few neighbours – picked men, carrying medical supplies, nourishment and waterproof covering – back up the gorge down which I had brought the news, the shortest way to the wreck. The doctor was to come out by car to Stephens's, and their party was to cross a narrow divide into Christmas Creek gorge where I was to meet them at half -past two that night.

What a splendid thing in the moments of greatest emergency to have a man like Bob Stephens to lean on! Bob was a captain in the A.I.F. Quick, constructive thinking is a habit of his, and obstacles are made for him to overcome. What a splendid thing, too, to have had on call John Buchanan, with his quiet confidence, the one man in the world I would have picked to lead that cutting party through fourteen miles of soaking green Hell, without visibility or even the sun as a guide.

The plan made, we rushed on to the township of Hillview, to organise the trackcutting party, and to get all available brushhooks and axes, food for an army of men, and packhorses to get everything to the Plateau.

To the safe keeping of the postmistress, Gracie Silcock, I gave poor Westray's mildewed wallet. To Gracie must go most of the credit for getting together the volunteers. She stuck to her telephone all night, calling numbers, explaining where to go and what to take, and all this in between floods of incoming press and radio calls and "long distances" from incredulous relatives and friends. I rushed to the store and ordered incredible amounts of bread, butter, tea and sugar and tinned food – a final thought was a large quantity of flat files for sharpening brush hooks. Swiftly time flies when moments are precious; here was half past one, and I had to rush off for my two-thirty rendezvous with the doctor's party. I had thought to get a change of clothing to replace my wet things, but there hadn't been time. It didn't matter, anyhow, because rain had started again before midnight. Heavy drenching showers driven down the gorge from the mountains on a strong, cold wind; cold rain that would be making extra hell for those poor devils backup on that high range where the temperature would be ten degrees lower.

The horses were caught again, and we went off into the dark at half gallop. Suddenly, the horses reared and plunged as the powerful headlights of a car shot over a hill behind us. It was the first press car, and they wanted a statement and a flashlight photograph, but there were men higher up who needed brandy more than these fellows needed their copy, so I gave my brief apologies, and galloped on, on past the region of cars, plunging through the deep creek crossing, iron horseshoes clattering on submerged rocks, past the last trace of civilisation to where the gorge closed in and the big timber began; on, until a fire shining dimly through trees and falling rain, showed that the doctor's party had beaten me to the spot.

Greetings were taken for granted; Billy cans were on the fire, and near the boil. Here was my first look at Dr. Lawler, a well-made young man, who looked as though he could stand the frightful gruelling which I knew was ahead of him. His professional work began sooner than he expected; I was in need of some small attention. The pause before the billies boiled gave me a chance to strip off my sodden, stinking clothes and wash some of my fatigue away in the icy water of the creek. Then the billies were boiling and we were scalding our mouths with good old tea. It is funny how hot tea can shoot warmth through a cold wet body, and yet in a heat wave can be more cooling than ice water. As the Cornishman said of his ale: "In summer it do cool 'ee down, and in winter it do warm 'ee up."

There is still a clear mental picture of the men standing with their mugs of tea; their faces shown strongly in the firelight had a queer strained look – steam curled up from their sodden clothes, large drops rained down from the leaves of a huge Moreton Bay fig overhead, hissing into the hot ashes. For yet another night and two more days, that band was still together, still in wet clothes, still without sleep, but with faces that had aged ten years.

Now we were under way. A fantastic file of lanterns and torches. The introduction was a strong one for the party – a creek crossing a chain wide and thigh deep, floored with slimy boulders like pumpkins, but there were miles of that ahead. We came out of the stream bed, and slashed into a thorny wall of raspberry and wild ginger, across great wet logs six feet high. Back to the stream bed again, and then we tried our luck on the opposite side; got on to the side of a cliff before we knew it, got down to *terra firma* on vines, and started on up the creek bed again. Over and around the slimy boulders, as large as bales of wool, rain water trickling between our shoulder-blades, and creek water washing about our thighs. Now and then, a man would fall full length in the water, and Lawler, throwing aside his bedside manner would yell: "Mind that bottle of ether." Language, the only outlet for our feelings, was getting a lot thicker as we went.

By fitful lantern and torchlight, I got some idea of the torrent bed which I had traversed in darkness earlier that night. Earlier that night! Could it have been the same evening? Surely, it must have been twelve months ago, and two years since I left home! Came wet, grey daylight, and here speed was possible. In my pocket was a fresh clean handkerchief – borrowed – which I spread over poor Westray's face. He was gently carried from the creek to the mystic circle of trees where he now lies. We went on, a very silent band now. Time ceased to be. One slippery boulder was like another – one fall was like another – one hour like another. Even the strongest were showing strain. My legs had to be driven, forced like things that were almost dead, but there were no complaints now; over these boulders and around these waterfalls Westray had dragged his broken body. Away up above, without shelter in the cold driving rain, were two tortured, dying men, who could still joke on the eleventh day after the crash. God forgive me if I ever complain again.

It was about three o'clock when we left the camp fire. Ten o'clock found us still climbing over slippery boulders in the creek bed. The country between the wreck and the open country where I had gone, helldriven, in three hours, took eight hours to retrace. Bob and I got to the wreck first.

Briefly, he shook hands with the two men, and then, in his practical way, set to work building a fire without a second glance at the wrecked machine. My haversack was off and brandy, eggs and milk were whipped up in a pannikin. "Only a tablespoon full each, every ten minutes," Lawler had warned. "This is what I should have had for you yesterday," was my apologetic remark. "It was worth waiting for," said Joe Binstead.

Some time later, the doctor and the rest of the party being a little distance away, I disregarded the ten minute rule and gave the men an extra quick one before handing over to Lawler. The doctor, wan and exhausted, did not pause a moment to rest, but went straight to work on Proud's leg. Gordon Stephens rushed off for more water from Binstead's little creek – the doctor needed lots of hot water. Less than an hour later he told me confidently that Proud's life and limb would be saved. The very maggots which seemed to make the case so hopeless had eaten away the gangrenous flesh and checked the spread of fatal infection. Nature, with her own antiseptic, had protected a man beyond the reach of medical aid. I was to find out later that during the Great War many a Digger's life had been saved by flies.

A track was swiftly cut to the top of the Plateau, and a little tentlike shelter large enough for the two men, was erected. Thin, strong saplings were cut, threaded through chaff bags, and lashed to crosspieces with clothesline rope, to form stretchers. By early afternoon, the men were in their new home, sleeping with the aid of sedatives.

In the meantime, others of the party had made a start to cut the track back along the range top, to meet John Buchanan's cutting party. Lack of visibility and a crescent-shaped creek gorge threw our men out of their reckoning, but contact was made with the other party about sunset. Many of Buchanan's men had gone back towards civilisation for the night, but a band of men with Sid Smith in its van came through to our camp. Sid, himself an old Digger, who worked like a tiger and swore like a bullock driver, looked, as did the others, like a man who had done five day's work without resting, and that was about right too – they had done five day's work in one; they had worked with the savage desperation of miners whose mates are entombed; they had worked for a Cause, the divine spark which turns men into supermen.

Later, around dark, many more men came and joined the group about our smoky fires; prominent among these was the bearded, long-haired figure of Charles Burgess, the Hermit of Lamington, who did splendid scouting work that day for Buchanan's party. The Hermit dwells in a cave down on

Christmas Creek, and lives almost entirely on corn which he grows, grinds into meal with a little handmill and bakes on the coals in unleavened cakes. The one great precept of his simple religion is "Thou shalt not kill", and this he carries out so thoroughly and sincerely that he refuses to wear leather boots, because they involve the killing of animals.

I can say, without hesitation, that that night was the worst in my life. Two smoky sodden fires for thirty wornout men, no shelter from the wind and rain which redoubled as night fell; it seemed years since I had felt warmth, or had dry clothes on my body. Nobody made any pretence of trying to sleep. Most of the men stood up all night. And all the time I was sunk in the pit of misery and dejection, the outside world was shouting my name and frenzied journalists were searching for new words to describe my feat of bushcraft. Bushcraft! What a poor overworked word that became. Any person who has studied the topography and vegetation of the McPhersons would know that no matter how thoroughly he was equipped with bush instinct, a man might search there unsuccessfully for fifty years. This fact should be noted, and due credit given to my mother, who was saying her prayers back home.

Back home! What was happening? I tried to imagine, and then gave up. I was not to know that even then Viola and Rose were riding in the dark and wet up the slippery slopes of Lamington Plateau on the freshly cut track towards us. Rose, with her trained nurse's experience to assist Dr. Lawler if necessary, Viola to look after me. The word had reached home at half past ten on Sunday night, I heard later, and soon the household was up and about. Joe ran up to Goblin Wood to tell Viola; he woke her and lost his voice and could not say a word. Nobody could sit down or keep still, shock rather than excitement was their condition. But in all this excitement Mother's remained the one cool head. She calmly set about building up the dead fire, and made tea for the excited ones. Soon our house was flooded with telephone calls in much the same way as was Hillview. Nearly all of these calls were erroneously made by people who believed the O'Reilly Guest House to be the scene of events, instead of being far removed from them. Viola, Molly and Rose took relays at the telephone until morning.

And then with the morning, Viola, Rose and Mary Doherty set out on their ponies for the long wet ride across the lowlands. Instead of tackling the two day trip through the ranges on foot, they rode down the Stockyard Creek track, thence across the cleared foothills to Christmas Creek above Lamington. Many times on the way they passed dairy farms, deserted when their owners rushed off in the night to the rescue. Here were unmilked cows restless with their bulging milkbags and poddy calves which bellowed for food. Once Rose stopped to lift a little weak calf out of a pen and restore him to his fretting mother over the fence. Darkness caught them long before they reached the depot at the foot of the Plateau where the ambulance cars waited. It was from there, after some food and a rest at a log fire, that they set out again in the small hours on that dark and dangerous journey. They, too, had not slept in two nights, and it was fitting, I think, that they should have been the only women folk to get right on to the job and share in the hardships of the rescuers.

The latecomers to our fire had brought news that an army of men was assembling at the foot of the range to help with the work next day, Tuesday. A canteen had been established there by local women workers and a prominent firm of storekeepers in Beaudesert sent, free of all charge, a large truck load of provisions to feed the rescue party. They told, too, of an army of newspaper reporters and photographers, Movie newsreel men, radio announcers and experts, and a host of people who were there in the capacity of sightseers.

About an hour before dawn, Bob called for volunteers to carry Billy water for breakfast. An atmosphere of cheerfulness spread about through the men; partly at the prospect of tea and tucker, but mainly, I think, because of the proximity of daylight, and action. As we were drinking down the last of the tea, the bronze cuckoos commenced their pre-dawn wailing, and a faint grey light showed between the slits in the tree tops. A deluge just before the light came eased off, and allowed us to take down the waterproof coverings and arrange them across the stretchers. Then came the yellow robins ringing "chop, chop!" and with it the strong light. Steadily and without fuss, big strong men took their places; the word was quietly passed, and first Binstead's and then Proud's stretcher started off along that little tunnel which led for fourteen miles through the wet, green tangle. The last phase of the big work had commenced.

Bob, Charlie Steinhardt, Charles Burgess and I started ahead with our brush hooks, slashing loose vines and spikes which might trip the carriers; behind the stretchers came the reserve men, carrying food, and odds and ends of gear. There was no stopping for a rest. When a man tired, another took his place; the cavalcade kept moving. Around the bend ahead came a number of rain-sodden men; the leader, a tall chap with a drooping hat and a wet cornsack over his shoulders. He strode forward and grabbed my hand. He was brother Herb. Something caught inside me. I choked and said nothing. The men behind him were my cobbers from Kerry. They hadn't much to say, but the feel of their hard hands was good at a moment when I felt like "selling out cheap". They had been cutting on the previous evening and had spent the night under a Beech tree a few miles back. Another mile of slashing, and dimly round a bend through the rain came two familiar ponies. One a cream and the other a blue-grey. There was no mistaking them – Roufe and Blue Boy – our stocky half-brothers from home.

In the dim light, the ponies were more easily recognised than their riders, but I knew, before I could see clearly that they must have been Viola and Rose.

Although I was hatless, Viola would have passed me without recognition, such was the change that the few days had made. They had telegrams: one for Binstead and three for me. They had ridden off from the camp fire down by the ambulance cars at two in the morning, and after five hours riding, mostly through the dark, they came up with us.

Viola had started out with dry clothes for me, but the bottom had ripped out of the saddle bag in the timber and the clothes, together with their provisions, had fallen by the wayside, but nobody cared. Rose gave me her knitted jumper, and even over my wet things it made a great difference to my comfort.

In charge of Proud's stretcher was John Rosser, whose ceaseless vigilance and commands of "higher left," "lower back"; or "higher front," kept the stretchers always perfectly level and relieved any strain from the injured man's leg.

John Rosser was the unsung hero of a drama which stirred our district in 1931. Very early one morning in October of that year, little James Doyle, aged 19 months, strayed away from his parents' home on the Albert River above Kerry. By evening over a hundred people had joined the search which went on for two nights and two days. On the second day an aeroplane searched, but unsuccessfully. Rose and I spent two days and nights of fruitless tramping. On the second night Rose had a nasty experience. She was searching alone on a lonely flat up Lefthand River, when she saw in the light of the half moon two big dingoes tearing a small body on the ground. She drove the dingoes away and then found to her relief that they had been eating a freshly killed calf. On the second morning, over fifty hours after he had disappeared, little James was found by John Rosser, just in the nick of time. The toddler had travelled over five miles and had crossed a rugged range.

Something I shall never forget was my meeting that morning with the two brothers of Captain Boyden. We exchanged handshakes and a few words under the streaming trees. It was as unforgettable as the afternoon, a week later, when I met his mother.

One may readily understand the gratitude of the

rescued men, and the feelings of people when dear ones they have mourned as lost have come back from the grave. The most touching thing in the whole sad affair was the gratitude of the mother and brothers of Rex Boyden, and the mother and the young wife of James Westray; gratitude for definite word of their lost ones, and in the knowledge that they had had a Christian burial.

About midmorning, while carrying Proud's stretcher, I stumbled badly twice. I was relieved at once. Only willpower had been keeping me together, and now with extra help arriving every moment, and the end of the job in sight, the old legs refused duty.

Quickly we were joined by other groups of wet and worn men from the previous day's cutting party, their faces and hands and arms torn with lawyer and wild raspberry. One man who looked "all in" was Digger Jack Bishop. I especially remember too, big Bill Hayes, of Hillview – himself a tiger on the football field, who was a tower of strength to the party.

In the course of this story, I have mentioned the names of men here and there as they come into the narrative, but there are thirty and more whose names should range alongside, who took an equal part in the hardship and backbreaking toil and whose share in the glorious work will never be forgotten. And where will you find better men than those who carried the stretchers from the top of the Plateau, down and down, and right down that last steep range to the waiting ambulance cars below? The men in front, with the stretcher bars held above their heads; the ones at the back with the bars below their knees in order that the sick men should be kept on an even keel. At one point where the mountain broke away sharply, a stout rope was put around an entire stretcher party and anchored to another group of men, who steadied them down the declivity.

Slowly and resolutely, the carriers tramped down the last long slope; down at last to where the creek flat swelled up to meet the ridge.

ॐ

Let us draw the curtain for a moment, while the men who came back from the grave are restored to their families.

And then, eleven hours after that start in the grey of dawn, Binstead and Proud were put into the ambulance cars; the big job was done.

ॐ

I feel that some comment should now be made on what has been said regarding the cause of the disaster.

It has been suggested in some circles that the pilot was flying too low. That is very unfair. If you trace the course of the airliner from where it was last seen to where it crashed, you would find it crossed two ranges both higher than where the crash occurred. What is the answer? – the plane was forced down. It is a cowardly and despicable thing that irresponsible, ill-informed people should attempt to fasten blame on a man who cannot come forward to give an account of his stewardship. I do not wish to include within the scope of these remarks, men who had to give evidence under oath – naturally they were compelled in conscience to tell the truth as they thought it to be; rather these words are intended for unthinking people who would lightly seek to take away the reputation of a man who was a splendid airman.

Boyden was no amateur; he learned his flying in that hardest of schools, the Great War, and the men who went up in those flimsy crates and faced von Richthofen's guns were not wanting in either courage or skill. He lost his plane and his life in battling with Queensland's oldest and greatest enemy, the cyclone. What is a light aeroplane to a cyclone? Cities have been razed in such winds. Who remembers the Yongala and the Waratah, two great steel ships which disappeared with all hands? No trace of them was ever seen.

Here is some information for which we are indebted to Gordon Stephens who lives in the last house up the Albert River under the shadow of Mt. Widgee and directly in the line of flight of the Stinson that day. Gordon is a keen observer and I have every confidence in his opinion, also he was one of the last people to see the plane in flight. He states that at the time the aeroplane flew over there were two levels of cloud; one a smother of low white cloud which partly concealed Mt. Widgee and poured down through the gorges completely hiding the high backbone of ranges beyond. The other was the ceiling of the cyclone itself; this he estimated to be at least fifteen hundred feet above Mt. Widgee. As the plane went over still climbing, its wings were seen to cut into the high ceiling and it finally disappeared into that bank. Since

Mt. Widgee is well above three thousand feet, this would place the altitude of the plane above Stephens's at little short of five thousand feet, and it was obvious to him by the sound of its motors that it was still climbing. Even at the same height at which it passed over Gordon's house, the plane would have cleared the point where the wreck occurred, by nearly two thousand feet.

And that is why the Stephens brothers and their immediate neighbours who were the last people to see the plane in flight did not consider for one moment that it could have got into difficulties over the McPhersons. To understand the manner of down-draught which caused the disaster, it would be necessary to understand a little of the geography of the McPherson Range; on the southern side from which the cyclone blew at its greatest velocity, the range rises from low coastal country in great sheer ramparts for from three to four thousand feet. The cyclone, striking full against these mighty walls was forced up in a great arc at more than a hundred miles an hour. It is an established scientific fact that the descending section of this arc has even greater velocity. Back a few yards from the edge of the cliff, where the wind screamed like a thousand demons, was a dead calm in which it would be possible to light a cigarette with ease. Ample proof of the destructive force of the down-draught is given by the fact that the trees along the main top of the range had barely a leaf disturbed, while in the bottom of sheltered gorges half a mile back on the northern side, the destruction of timber almost passed description.

There has been something on my mind since the crash, and this seems to be the place to say it.

We all know that the safety of aviation has been built upon the lessons of a thousand disasters. What then, is the lesson of the Lamington crash? To me it seems this. There should be at each great aerodrome a disinterested official (preferably a Government official) with full knowledge of wind and air conditions along immediate air routes: This official should have power to ground a plane if, in his opinion, the occasion warrants it. I am not suggesting here that such a state of affairs would have prevented the Stinson crash, but is it fair that a pilot whose job is such an exacting one, should have the added responsibility of deciding whether or not a passenger plane should go up in bad weather? There are too many factors which may cloud his judgment; keeping faith with his passengers who expect to get through; loyalty to his company which has a splendid all weather flying record, and lastly the old slogan, "The air mail must go through." It seems to me that the final decision should rest with someone who owes no loyalty to the service.

People have asked me why Westray attempted to climb down those cliffs which he knew to be dangerous – the answer is simple; the cliffs were between him and civilisation, and men of Westray's stamp do not turn back from a job because it becomes dangerous. He had gone for help, and for him there was no turning aside from his purpose. He had already negotiated country far more difficult than where he fell – cliffs which I found to be extremely dangerous, and I was not handicapped by two badly burnt hands.

Of all the ravine beds which I have traversed in the National Park area, that which Westray had to travel down was the worst. It would seem that the fire demons in making it had done everything their spite could conceive. Between towering volcanic cliffs was the stream bed, choked with great blocks of lava, green with slime and moss. Here and there huge trees had been torn from the cliffs by the cyclone, their heads smashed into the gorge, but their great trunks were wedged upright along the cliffs – there was not room for them to fall into the choked stream bed. Everything seemed to be conspiring against the rescue; time was going – "If I don't get out of this gorge tonight, Proud will die before help comes," was my thought. It must have been just after the place where Westray fell, that I lost my head and began to run and leap across the gaps between the slimy lava blocks – if I'd slipped, I too would have been smashed up and help would never have got to the men, but, I thought, as far as I was capable of thinking, that they would die, anyhow, if I didn't get help that night.

It is like a dream now, that wild run. I was quite mad – my heart had been wrung out with horror and with pity – no one who looked upon those poor survivors could help praying as I did that God would let me live long enough to help these men. I knew that I was sobbing and that I only paused when tears blinded me. I remember too, that the shock and jar of leaping and landing on these rocks at top speed was telling on me, even though I was in splendid condition, but I was given strength to complete the task.

Part Two

CHAPTER IV

Family Life in Kanimbla Valley

THE year 1902 was a memorable one in the history of pastoralists. At that time my family lived in the Kanimbla Valley, New South Wales, and my brother Tom, still the finest chap I've ever known, told me many things about that dreadful winter. The ice, even at noon, blocked the ripples of the creek, and there were over sixty hard frosts in succession, frosts which killed big gum trees on Round Ridge and Blackfellow's Hill. It was Australia's worst year of drought, and the tall oaks which lined the creek banks like an avenue of Lombardy Poplars had to be lopped to provide feed for the starving sheep.

The desperately needed rain came in September,

1903, just at the time I was born. Our home was a little slab house on Long Swamp Creek. Long Swamp Creek flows east from the Divide near Jenolan Caves, and is gravely misnamed, in that it is quite a short creek and has not sufficient marsh land to deserve the libel of being called a swamp. It crosses the southern portion of Kanimbla Valley to join Cox's River, that mild-looking stream which, in angry flood, becomes the swiftest and most treacherous river in New South Wales.

Through our property Long Swamp ran as a placid brown stream over gravel beds; knee deep in good seasons, ankle deep in drought time, floating with yellow leaves in autumn, fringed with ice in winter. Alive with tadpoles, eels, and an occasional spikyfinned carp, it provided a bathing, wading, and fishing ground which later experience of the finest surf beaches of Australia can never dim. In September the silver wattles shed their golden bloom and breathe the sweetest fragrance of the bushland along the creek, and the weeping willows, after their long winter sleep, dip their ropes of tender green buds into the friendly shallows. Such was Long Swamp at my advent, and I wonder if that is the reason wattles in bloom and willows in leaf bud still have a poignant meaning for me.

Let me here pay tribute to the wonderful pluck and spirit of the women of Australia's bushland, who, as in the case of my own birth, far away from any medical or nursing assistance, went through such critical periods with no help but a neighbour's, giving a like service in return. We rightly remember our War heroes, but I would like to see in the growing art of our country, a greater recognition of the pioneering women who bred and reared the sturdy men and women of this continent. Here is an instance of the many demands made on their endurance. The rainfall already referred to, brought forth the greatest coat of grass in local memory. A few months later this made fuel for the most devastating bush fire in the history of our part of the country.

Black New Year – a day always to be remembered!

The bush fire had been burning sullenly on the Great Divide to the west and south of us for more than a week, burning steadily about three feet high through underbrush and rank grass.

Tom, Herb and Norb went off on Christmas Day to fight a fire which was already threatening Cousin Bob's sheep run, Kiangatha. Norb was only a lad of fourteen, but active and tough as a wallaroo. Mother was anxious about her boys; she too was born in Kanimbla Valley and none knew better that a bush fire could twist in a treacherous wind and burn men to death before they could run fifty yards. Fighting a fire which is confined to one city block is a dangerous enough business but when a bushfire comes on a thirty mile front across a thousand square miles of country, dry as tinder, then death walks very close to men who try to impede its progress.

Boxing Day brought more trouble. Ann, then six years old, running wild with her Christmas toys, fell and broke an arm; it was a compound fracture, and a jagged bone protruded through the flesh. A fine old bearded neighbour, Mick Cullen, brought 'his sulky (we had none) and drove the five hours' journey to Lithgow, while Dad held Ann in his arms. The midsummer heat, aided by bushfires, had sent the temperature soaring away above the century mark and had badly affected Ann's arm; it was black before they got to Lithgow. The doctor wanted to amputate it at once, but agreed to wait until morning. Dad was in an agonising position, fire was threatening his home and his boys were in the thick of the fighting, but he had to stay in Lithgow, where a child's life might depend upon the decision he made. He called in another doctor who ordered the arm to be packed in ice; for three weeks the ice packs were kept on until the inflammation went down sufficiently to allow the arm to be set, and for three weeks Ann's life was in danger. In the meantime Dad had hurried home.

About fifty men of the district had been working day and night to keep the fire in subjection. Fire trails four feet wide and many miles long were scraped clean of leaves and twigs; these trails were patrolled so that when a burning tree fell across; the new fire was beaten out with bushes. There is no harder work than fighting bush fires; constant heat up to 150 degrees, bitter smoke which made the strongest men collapse and gasp on the ground (there is nearly always a stratum of pure air up to four inches above the ground), searing smoke which made every moment of the day one of torture for the eyes. Added to all that was the ever present possibility of a big wind rising suddenly; if this happened all the fighters would be trapped and incinerated.

At night Mother and the other women, neighbours' wives and daughters, carried provisions out to the men, while Molly looked after the little people back at the house. There was no need of a light, a chain of fire stretched for thirty miles across the Black

Range, Alum Mount, and the Great Divide; the countryside and sky were lit almost as brightly as day, but the light was blood red.

It was shortly before dawn on the last day of the old year that the big wind began to rise, it came lightly and fitfully at first. All knew what it meant; there was no longer any question of keeping the fire in subjection; it was every man for himself. They raced down out of the mountains and made for their own clearings to try to save houses and stock. Some of them who lived distances away did not reach home; the fire, travelling finally above sixty miles an hour when the wind reached full velocity, bore down on them; they found clearings and submerged themselves in water. Miles ahead at their homes, perhaps a wife and little children lay in wet blankets in the middle of a newly ploughed cultivation paddock – all that had saved them. Kiangatha was the first to go, homestead and all. Bob lost all his sheep. The bulk of them, splendid fat fellows, were burned against a fence in one little gully; the blazing grease from their carcases ran a quarter of a mile down the hill.

Dad and the boys rushed our sheep into a small green grass paddock which would not burn.

Large numbers of wallabies, driven before the fire, joined our stock in the little sanctuary. So great was their fear of the fire that they lost all fear of man, their natural enemy.

Casks of water were drawn from the creek; the thatched roofs of the house and the bark shed were thoroughly soaked; in spite of this precaution the house roof caught fire three times. All the little ones, together with clothes and some household treasures, were taken to the creek. The thermometer stood at 130 degrees but that was as high as it would register.

At last it came; there was a roar more terrible than anything they had yet heard; the sun was blackened out, the light faded into awful twilight through which was a sullen red glow; the wind became a hail storm of sparks and fluffy, blazing stringybark. The fire, travelling in great tongues one hundred feet above the treetops leaped over the hill into our back paddock. Here suddenly occurred one of those vagaries of the wind which some might construe as coincidence, but which we choose to think of as the answer to ardent family prayers. When the fire was only two hundred yards beyond the shed, the wind suddenly dropped to a mere breeze, and, deprived of its forced draught, it dropped back to earth and hissed along through grass and bushes no faster than a man could walk. Mother, Dad and the boys, inspired by the hope of saving the house, rushed with their bushes and wet bags to beat out the blazing line; they stood and beat, retreating when the breeze freshened and attacking when it calmed; beat, to fall when smothered with heat and smoke, gasp a lungfull of sweet air from the ground level, and rise to beat again.

Sometimes Mother left the battle to run to the creek to see how her baby and small ones fared; they were quite comfortable up to their necks in water with wet muslin over their heads for protection against the fiery rain which fell over the countryside as at Pompeii.

It is easy to imagine that through all the battle and anxiety Mother's mind seldom left little white-face Ann, lying in Lithgow Hospital. That day was

Mother's birthday, and I wonder if ever a bush mother had a more trying one.

Safe in our little sanctuary in that blackened countryside our family watched the fire cross Long Swamp. Then the wind screamed to a hurricane again, its velocity increased through the afternoon, and the fire rushed along Megalong Valley in great sheets of flame which reached out across clearings, taking homes at one lick, and leaving only the water storage tanks, boiling like great kettles. Up through the big gum country to the Blue Mountains it screeched, borne by a wind of seventy miles an hour, with walls of flame two hundred feet above the treetops – even the creeks in its path boiled dry.

The worst of our battle lasted less than an hour; the fire had been diverted around the buildings and the orchard; thirty acres of grass had also been saved, a small help to the stock until more grew; but the battle had not been won by any means. All day the flying sparks caused fresh outbreaks in our little oasis, even on the buildings themselves. All hands remained on guard far into the night, their clothes riddled with holes from burning sparks. Around, the hills glowed like a forge and hollow trees spouted flame like the fountains of hell. Every so often a great dead gum, blazing inside and out, would fall high up on the rocky tops, and there would be an avalanche of fire down the side of Marsden's Rock.

Such were the events of the first year of my life.

Two years later I began to take definite notice. My earliest memory is of my first riding lesson on an old chestnut mare named jenny. I was sitting in the saddle somewhat fearfully and Jenny was being led around the shed. Then came summer days of wading in the creek, catching tadpoles and making pools for them in scooped out sand; swinging out and back on hanging willow ropes. Across the creek, through a rabbitproof fence, was Redfern Hill, a bare, granite ridge dotted with stunted prickly bushes which yielded edible, slightly sweet berries, affectionately known as "puddens". Rose (two years older) took me on many a feeding excursion, braving with our small bare feet hot granite sand, milk thistles and colourful, but thorny, Mexican Poppies. In between the cracks of granite rocks lived black and yellow horrors – lizards – known as "Rock Adders," reputed to be deadly poisonous (a libel which they have lived down). But anyhow, we kept very wide of them and gingerly threw stones at extreme range, without ever scoring a direct hit.

Our house was a four-roomed one with a verandah to the north-east; the slabs were of split stringy bark two feet wide and fastened vertically by cleats top and bottom. Where the slabs fitted unevenly, narrow strips of galvanised iron were tacked on to cover up the cracks. The floors were of slabs smoothed by an adze smoothed too by many comings and goings of other little feet before mine. There were no glass windows – instead there were large wooden shutters, hinged at the top, which were propped out and up by sticks and were let down only under extreme conditions of weather; the hinges were simply strips of leather – disused harness straps. The main room off the verandah was a kitchen, living and dining room; across the whole of one end was a great fireplace usually accommodating a back log, so large that it took two men to carry it in. On either side of the fire a hob ran along the wall and it was possible for the whole family to sit inside the fireplace on a cold night. Over the fire hung chains and hooks to support boilers, kettle and camp oven. The great hearth was paved with flat slabs of ironstone which Dad had brought from the back paddock. Inside, the walls of the house were covered with hessian over which was pasted layer upon layer of newspaper; the paste used was ordinary cooking flour mixed with water. The final coat of paper to go on was usually of pictorial pages from the *Sydney Mail* and the *Town and Country Journal*, pride of place being reserved for their coloured Christmas supplements. Without any purpose other than to make the room cosy in the only attractive way possible, many historical scenes and figures of the late Victorian era were scattered about our walls and mellowed into soft, brown tones by occasional back draughts of smoke from the hearth. More coloured supplements were added as the Christmas seasons went by. Clearest in my memory is a slightly smoked print of Lambert's masterpiece, "Across the Blacksoil Plains"; I have only to close my eyes now to see those splendid horses straining. I was twenty years of age when I saw the original in the Sydney Art Gallery.

Outside was a huge garden which was commonly called "The Yard". It was entirely without order. With apparently no premeditated plan, trees and shrubs were scattered about – box and privet, poplars, alders, oleanders and many lilacs. Scented vines and English ivy draped the old split paling fence. Dad was an idealist who grew plants and shrubs because he loved to grow them, not because they made neat, coloured, geometrical patterns in the garden. Dad's run was not very good country nor highly productive, so, to add to the little family treasury, he went on many droving trips. Never once did he return without his saddle bags stuffed with seeds, cuttings and roots collected in perhaps three hundred miles of homeward riding. Jogging along with his packhorse, he would see a lady working in a beautiful garden; he would ride up to the fence, admire her garden and ask questions about this plant or that. At the time horticulture was not a usual accomplishment amongst men of the Outback. The lady, intrigued by the knowledge of this low-voiced, bearded drover, would keep conversation going for an hour or more while the packhorse picked along the way untended. Later, when Dad took the road he would have been comfortably filled with tea and cakes while the pockets of his old velvet corded coat bulged with little parcels of precious seeds. Should it have been evening he most likely would have met the master of the house and been asked to stay the night.

Those were lonely days, not only in company but in news and communications; an agreeable stranger to talk to was a gift from the gods. For Dad's part, given tobacco and a log fire, he was never happier than when yarning into the small hours. The host would have been free to choose his own subjects; Dad's range was unlimited. Judged by modern standards he was an uneducated man, but he was a keen observer and much of his reading was natural science and poetry with some Greek mythology thrown in for good measure. He knew the constellations and always kept up to date with the phases of the planets. It is easy to remember him now looking up at that old blackened mantle clock – which looked like the facade of a wooden cathedral – and saying "Nine o'clock, about time Jupiter was up"; then we would follow him outside, shivering, and watch while the great white jewel pushed itself up through the skeleton network of dead trees on Redfern Hill. Dad's astronomy was not all learned from books. His youth and early manhood were spent stock riding and droving on the vast plains of the Inland where homesteads were fifty to one hundred miles apart, where a man might ride a thousand miles and more without crossing a fence or a made road or seeing one hill which would serve as a land mark; where the sun, moon and stars were the only guide posts to save him from one of the three inevitable ends of lost men – thirst, starvation or a firehardened spear. To the western men of that era, astronomy was a very exacting science with death the penalty of ignorance.

There was an orchard down on a small loam flat by the creek; it was bounded by an irregular log fence which followed, on one side, the windings of Long Swamp. There were many trees: apples, pears, quinces, plums, cherries, peaches, figs; all planted with the soothing irregularity which characterised the garden, but all were fruitful and well cared for. The orchard had but one touch of Dad's playful genius, a cherry tree which forked into three boughs each bearing a different kind of fruit.

Many of the slab houses in our district looked very neat with their coats of whitewash or kalsomine; ours had no colouring, the slabs being left in their natural state, but the years had mellowed them to a restful, silver-grey and mottled them with pale green lichen. At the far end of the verandah, screened by Churchyard Ivy, hung a canvas bag full of drinking water from Long Swamp; it was cold and sweet with the subtle flavour of canvas. Our water storage was a fifty gallon cask mounted on a slide; when empty our draught horse, Bloss, was harnessed and the slide towed down a winding cart track to the "dipping hole" under the willows.

With the cargo aboard, Bloss plodded back up the grade, leaving a wet trail all the way; the cask came to rest again under the big acacia tree by the steps and so we had water for another day.

A homemade wooden settee stood on the verandah; here in slack times, Dad sat while he plaited wonderful greenhide stock whips which were the envy of his neighbours. They were stout whips, built to endure and in the hands of stockmen they boomed like a twelve gauge shotgun; he gave many away, and one, the last he made, is still doing good service twenty-five years later. Above the settee hung his thermometer which was read regularly; its yellow paint was blistered near the bulb – Mick could have told you why. It happened one day of bitter cold when we were grouped on the verandah edge watching the snow pile up on Table Rock and Minni Minni. All day the mercury had been shrinking back into the bulb like a snake going into hibernation. In by the hearth with its huge back log of yellow box sat Dad with a few bearded cronies who had decided that the day was not suitable for any occupation other than yarning by the fire. As we listened, they were arguing the point about whether the day was colder or warmer, than that other Wednesday back in 1884. "We'll soon settle that," said Dad, "Come out and read the glass." Stools and homemade chairs scraped on the floor as the men rose from the fire, and then Mick with one of those brainwaves which had earned him some doubtful fame, put a lighted match to the thermometer bulb; the mercury shot up like a jack-in-the-box and we shot round the corner to be out of sight but not out of hearing. There was some stamping about while spectacles were being adjusted, then a long bleak silence while the shocked group read the verdict, 130 degrees Fahrenheit. "Well I'll be...", said one. "Well strike me...", added another. "Well I go to...", said a third. "Those nippers have been at it again", said Dad, stamping back to thee fire. He never mentioned the incident to us but I am sure he enjoyed the joke; it was so much like what he himself would have done given an equal opportunity. Mick provided much of the humour of those early days but his practical jokes were often close to the wind and a bad end was predicted for him by more than one relative.

From the big shutter window on the verandah could be seen the white cart road winding away between the apple trees up Walker's Flat. It was from this window that Mother watched at night when the dread bushrangers, Jimmy Governor and his gang, were leaving their trail of murder and outrage across the bushland. News came only once a week and no one knew where the gang would strike next. Dad was away droving and Mother watched while a month old baby and the other little ones slept.

We had the loveliest old sheep dog – Lass. She is quite a dim memory, but she is something in the nature of a tradition in our family, and tales about her will be told so long as an O'Reilly survives. She was very old as I remember her. Her later years were devoted to rearing families of yapping, pot-bellied pups, which were the delight of our young lives. We remember her too, as our guardian when we played by the creek, always scouting for snakes and killing them when she found them. Her pup, Trixie, and Trixie's pup, Kitty, were also snake killers, so it must have been in the breed. I had good reason to remember Lass many years later when my own little girl, Rhelma, was running wild along a jungle track with her two cattle pups, Koko and Yum Yum, in the van. The pups stopped, put up their bristles and growled; Rhelma checked her mad career; right in front was a tiger snake flattened and ready to strike. Every bush child should have a dog.

The tales of Lass, of her cleverness and her faithfulness, would fill a book, which I may some day write; here I shall content myself with one. After the great bush fire, a number of neighbours assembled in the gorge beyond Marsden's Rock to repair boundary fences. When a boundary fence was burnt out, neighbours on each side shared in the labour of repairing it. Tom and Herb went along to do our share of the work and with them went Lass. The camp ran short of meat, so on the first evening a sheep was killed and hung well clear of the dogs on a little leaning tree. During the night, while the men slept, the tree broke under the strain. Morning saw Lass standing guard over the carcase, growling and fighting back half a dozen other dogs which would have torn it to pieces. The dead sheep was quite unmarked. It had been a cold night, and Lass must have been very hungry.

For many years Dad's sheep dogs had been the best in the district. How he got the first of the line is worth recording. For some years their origin was a mystery, even to Dad, but later he found out, and this is the story which is true in every detail. Somewhere in the `eighties – before Dad was married – one of the best known squatters of the Bathurst district imported some sheep dogs from Scotland. The dogs were reputed to be the best ever imported into the colony. Some months later they were exhibited in the Bathurst Show. One bitch had a litter of four puppies. Dad did not go to the Bathurst Show, as Bathurst was twelve hours ride distant. About midnight on the night of the Show there was a hammering on the door of his bark-roofed humpy. Dad came out sleepily to open up. Mechanically he hung the billy over the red coals, the first duty in bush hospitality. Outside, a heavily bearded man was holding a sweating, heaving horse. He was a bushranger, and had been a member of Gardiner's Gang.

"How is the billy, Peter?" he said.

"Nearly on the boil", said Dad, "and there's some damper and corn junk. There's a bit of hay in the shed for your moke, he looks puffed out." Soon the man came back after throwing some hay to his horse.

"I've got four mates with me. Can you feed them too?" asked the bushranger. "Bring them in," said Dad.

"Here they are," the man said, as he brought from the pockets of his overcoat four whining puppies. Dad gave some milk to the puppies, and then the stranger produced a flask from his pocket, and the two men shared some hot rum. The bushranger ate quickly, then collected the puppies and went off again into the darkness – he had many miles to go before dawn.

Next morning Dad was awakened by another sound. A little puppy was whining and sniffing at the cracks in the slab hut; the bushranger had paid for his meal. Some years went by before Dad learned the origin of the little whining morsel which was the first of Lass's line.

During my life I have heard much condemnation of the bushmen who befriended bushrangers. Even aside from the fact that most bushrangers were victims of a vicious system, this criticism is difficult for me to understand. The ruthless cut-throat Bedouins have their sacred Guest Law. Would you have less in the hospitable Australian pioneer? Should he betray a man who had shared his billy of tea? One question I would like to ask those critics is – why is it that amongst Australian men the name of Aaron Sherritt, the Kellys' betrayer, is more despised than that of Ned Kelly?

Wash days were fun. Sometimes we had a dear old darkie, Fanny, to do the washing. Fanny smoked a corncob pipe and spilled pipe ash into the tub as she worked. She told uncanny tales drawn from aboriginal lore of ghosts and devils, which came under the general heading of "gubba". When telling her gubba stories, she talked deep down in her throat with the intake of her breath, a trick which gave the tales a startlingly grotesque effect. The clothesline and tubs were down by the creek, under the weeping willows, so that the soiled clothes had to be carried down there. Each child carried a bundle tied up in a sheet, and felt suitably important. The whole of washing day was one of play for the little people. There was never a creek more friendly to children than Long Swamp. There was not one pool in its whole length where a small child might drown. Its bed was gravel, with no stones to hurt tiny feet. Hundreds of red or blue dragonflies skimmed the water like squadrons of a fairy air force.

Baking day was another event. Mother didn't have a stove – she had a huge oven of brick and stone which Dad had built for her. On baking days we were sent to collect quantities of bark from dead red gum trees. With this we stoked the fire inside the oven until the bricks began to glow. Then the fire and hot coals were drawn with a homemade scraper, and the big tins of dough were pushed into the place where the fire had just been. The result was bread with an even, deep-brown crust, and there has never been anything like it in my experience. Roast meat, too – joints of beef or mutton of our own killing, and geese, ducks or fowls, of which Mother always had plenty, were cooked to the same rich and mellow brown, and with a tenderness that no stove cooking can achieve. Whenever I am truly hungry from the sharp air of our mountain, I think of brown roast goose, the way Mother used to do it, surrounded with all kinds of vegetables from our garden, cooked in the gravy, and adding to its richness.

An event in our lives, too, was the coming from Sydney of Cousin Mary – with red hair, and about my age. She told of trams and the sea, the zoo and other wondrous things we had never seen, but she insisted on calling the creek "the sewer", and stones were "bricks" to her. One evening we gave her a riding lesson barebacked, on a chestnut mare named Angelina. Ann, Rose and I got on with her for company. Angelina cantered very smartly considering her handicap, but she caught sight of a haystack, which gave her ideas. A right-angled turn ended the riding lesson; tutors and pupil fell with a tangle of arms and legs into the soft barley grass.

Ann – two years older than Rose – mastered the art of setting a rabbit trap, so from then on we three had a new interest in life, and the night we caught our first rabbit remains a milestone in our lives.

It was a still night of hard frost; the last golden leaves from our willow trees had long since floated down to Cox's River, and the cornstalks had been cut from Triangle Paddock. Triangle was a cultivation flat in the V formed by the meeting of Long Swamp and Walker's Flat Creek, and there on a small mound that afternoon at sunset Ann had set the trap, whilst Rose and I stood by with big eyes. Just after tea that night, the shrill squeal of a trapped rabbit came from Triangle, and off we set, making various kinds of progress, according to the length of our legs. In response to a shrilly-voiced complaint, the girls waited for me by the old log fence, and on we went, barefoot, over the thistles and the frost. None of us had ever heard of Frank Buck, but we "brought 'em back alive", nor was Frank Buck half as proud of his first tiger.

CHAPTER V

The New Home

L ATER came a sad event. Tom went off one morning to go to the canefields of North Queensland to earn more money for the family. On that afternoon I wanted to go and join him, so set off through our back paddock as fast as my four year old legs would carry me. Some hours later, they found me howling my eyes out down in the timber by Merriman Creek. Merriman – that is a name that is ever in my memory down through the years.

Herbert went away north to join Tom. There they worked for two years in the canefields and the copper mines, earning money that was badly needed at home. The Christmas before they returned was a hard one; money was very scarce. Norbert, too was working away. Two days before Christmas – yes, in the middle of summer – cold rain began to stream down and snow fell on the mountains! On Christmas Eve the downfall continued and quite early in the morning a great roar from the granite gorge beyond Marsden's Rock told that Cox's River, in one of its bursts of fury was coming down with a solid wall of water twenty feet deep; the Cox nearly always came down that way, and faster than a man could run.

We were cut off from the Blue Mountains and the shop in Blackheath where our slender Christmas order had been placed. It was a grey, terrible day, a sodden earth and a sodden sky, and always the steady, cold rain, and always Cox's River roaring like the maddened monster that it was. Mother was ill, it was shortly before Joe was born; is there anything more sad or desolate than a home with a sick mother?

Tom had once swum the Cox in flood like that, after a cloudburst, with inches of hail floating on top, and racing logs, bigger than tiger sharks and just as dangerous. But Tom was beyond Cloncurry, nearly two thousand miles away. Night came on, and the family faced a cheerless Christmas; there would be none of those little luxuries which helped to make the Holy Day the happiest day of the year for bush people. Worse still, there were three little ones with implicit faith in Santa Claus, and three expectant stockings hung at the foot of a bed. It was almost the identical setting of Bret Harte's immortal Christmas story, How Santa Claus came to Simpson's Bar, but in our case there was no big, reckless, half drunken miner who faced a double death and a double temptation, so that a child's stocking might not be empty on Christmas morning.

Our story worked out in a different way. Molly, who had herself not long outgrown Santa Claus, could not bear the thought of those empty stockings. All night long she worked by the light of a smoky oil lamp, painting rainbow colours on old worn rubber balls, fashioning little toys and covering them with silver paper, making necklaces and bracelets with bright beads taken from milk jug covers, making toffee and parcelling it up in coloured paper. With the chill, wet dawn, three young people awakened to find stockings fat with mysterious parcels, and not all the toys of a millionaire's child could have made them happier that Christmas morning.

A week later, when the flats dried up and the river subsided, someone "found" a mysterious parcel of toys which must surely have been accidentally dropped from Santa's chariot. They were nice toys and we liked them, but none thought half as much of them as of those which came on Christmas Day.

After two years Herb and Tom came home with money to build us a new home; what a palace compared with our old slab house. The new building was rammed earth – p*isé de terre* it is called, a pre-Columbian American method – with walls two feet thick, cool in summer and warm in winter. A "bush carpenter", George by name, was called in to help my brothers with the woodwork, roof and plumbing, such as it was. George had a dexterous hand, a short temper, and, so it seemed to us, an unreasonable dislike for small children, who wallowed in the fragrant pine shavings under his feet, baulked his adze strokes, did some carpentering of their own with his soldering iron for a hammer, made large gaps in the razor-edges of his precious planes; or, to vary proceedings, would climb on to his benches or trestles and fall off, filling his workroom with that sound most beloved of crusty bachelors – the bawling of children.

When later the house was finished and George

had passed on to the realms of bogeymen, we found one of his old boots amongst the rank grass and nettles in a corner of the yard. Then we collected some gum sticks and burned the relic with a great show of unholy joy.

Long it was before the novelty wore from the new house – there were glass windows (we had had only wooden shutters before), but better than the windows were the two one thousand gallon tanks for the house water supply, which saved our daily task of bringing water from Long Swamp in the barrel.

Twice a week now the mailman came riding, just about dark, on the little track over the shoulder of Redfern Hill; and as soon as the tea things were cleared away there was a great rustling of newspapers, as Dad, after finding his glasses, settled down to read the *Lithgow Mercury* – his Bible, he called it – while we younger fry shouldered each other to look at the pictures in the *Sydney Mail,* and the elder brothers scrapped over the *Bulletin*, roaring loudly over the efforts of Livingstone Hopkins and the Lindsays, or the latest cartoon of Sir George Reid.

Should there happen to be any news out of the ordinary the mailman told us before putting his horse away, and I have a perfect recollection of hearing him tell in a suitably solemn voice of the death of Edward the Seventh.

One day Herb had been out in the back paddock, chasing out some of our neighbour's sheep which had got through a gap in the fence, and he came home to tell us of a new wild bees' nest which he had found in a hollow gum tree. That night the older brothers went out to rob it, taking a couple of axes and optimistically carrying a few empty kerosene tins for the honey and honeycomb which might be in the tree. We children went along to get in the way, and to be on the spot when the first honey came out of the hive. Off we went up the ridge, the hurricane lamps swinging and the tins rattling. It does not take a couple of big chaps long to chop down a hollow tree, and before the echoes of the crash died away we little people were running for our lives to get away from the bees, which, for some reason, seemed to be annoyed about everything.

Robbing bees' nests at night has one great advantage – the bees usually miss their target and finally settle down. Soon we came timidly back in time to collect big pieces of white honeycomb filled with clear, appletree honey. The party set off home again, the younger people carrying the lanterns and the older brothers lumping tins heavy with honeycomb. This was later put into cheesecloth, tied up plum pudding fashion, and hung up in the kitchen, a large dish being placed underneath to catch the pure honey which drained from the comb. Mother bottled it up next morning, and that day saw the pantry shelves lined with pickle bottles full, looking like rows of toy soldiers.

Shearing time was fun. It meant lots of extra men, excitement and wool and dust and tar. We used to try our hands at picking up fleeces when no one else was looking, but were quickly discouraged by thistle thorns and burrs hidden in the wool. A bullock team came to take away the wool and it was our practice to meet it a mile up the road and ride in on the flat waggon top. Bill, who drove the bullocks, had a slow, deep, drawling voice, and called the bullocks many unfamiliar words. Here

I pause to say something about Dad. About twice in my memory I heard him use that vicious word, "damn". It was not until I knocked about the world in after years that I realised that my Dad was one of the cleanest spoken of men.

Another regular event of great importance was the arrival of Jundah Singh, a Hindoo hawker, who came with a van full of secret sliding panels and drawers which contained goods that were to us comparable with the riches and mysteries of Jundah's native India. Apart from the display of his wares, we took a great interest in his cooking, and stood in an awe-stricken circle about his camp fire while he consumed an incredible number of hardboiled eggs and large quantities of curry, which, when sampled on one occasion, seemed to us as hot as molten lead. He often offered us curry on future occasions, but we had learned wisdom. One day I found myself with is 2d to spend. I bought a sliding pencil case from him, one of the old kind with coloured top. With the few pence left, I invested in a little tin of quince jam. On the shelves of Mother's pantry were many jars of the same variety of jam, and of a superior quality, but to me jam which came out of a tin with a pretty label was like a gift from another world.

Just before my fifth birthday came a lady teacher (weeks of fear and trembling had preceded her coming). Two miles up the creek, just halfway to our nearest neighbour, they were ramming the pisé walls for my first school; the work was all voluntary, and in about a fortnight there arose the prettiest lollycake house you ever saw! It had bright red earth walls and a thatched roof, which looked as if it had been stolen from an oversized beehive, two funny square windows and an odd-looking chimney. It just needed a few gnomes and a large toadstool to complete the fairy tale. The floor was of earth, and we sprinkled it each morning with water to keep down the dust. Twenty-five yards from the door the creek rippled and sang between smooth granite rocks and high reeds. Willows dipped into the pools and water dragons sunbaked on the rocks or dived with a loud "plop" into the water, as fancy took them. Magpies and leatherheads punctuated the lessons with their carolling, and in late spring built their nests and reared their families in the trees which shaded our playground. One pair of leatherheads borrowed from the school roof a piece of homemade, stringybark rope which was used for tying down the thatch; they used as much as they wanted for their purpose, and left the end hanging from the nest about ten feet. It was the oddest nest I've ever seen.

Wild birds were the greatest joy of my boyhood. Wild birds – and they're not so wild if you try to make friends with them – are, I think, the most beautiful of living things; the most sweet-voiced and the gentlest of creatures. They have been my neighbours and my very great friends all my life; and what wonderful neighbours they can be. They work the whole day through to combat insect pests; they build nests and feed large families of potential guardians of our crops, please the eye with flashes of glorious colour and sing to us the sweetest music in the world. There is one other great lesson which human neighbours could learn from bird neighbours, and this is why they are gentler and nicer than humans – they never say a cruel word about anyone. You may say that it is just because they cannot speak, but I know birds well enough to know that if they could talk, they would only say the nicest things. So next time you see a gentle feathered creature in a tree, just pause to think how inferior you are.

I can feel that some reader is itching to say – "Well, what about crows?" To that I would say, if the shades of Elbert Hubbard will forgive me, "There is so much good in the worst of 'crows', and so much bad in the best of 'humans,' that it ill becomes 'humans' to talk about 'crows'."

Without birds as our guardians, it would be impossible for agricultural and pastoral Australia to carry on, and if the birds do occasionally help themselves to some of our products, they are taking less than the just wages due to them. Australia's great agricultural problem, the grasshopper plague, is due to the killing of birds and the destruction of the trees which shelter them.

One other thing about birds which endears them to me is the way they help in times of sadness; and in times of joy make one feel still more joyous. Often when working alone in the jungle, cutting new tracks or clearing up cyclone debris, through lack of human company I fall to brooding over and magnifying my troubles, when my most beloved of birds, the yellow robin, comes saucily into the picture and alights on the side of a tree, perhaps about four feet from me and looks at me with head cocked on one side. Then he flies down to the ground and up on to the side of another tree, looks at me again with head tilted at a crazy angle. He never alights on anything horizontal – any fool bird could do that – and this little pantomime goes on until I laugh aloud, for it is impossible to mistake the warm friendship of the small creature. On the other hand, perhaps things are going well, and I have reason to be happy about everything. Then suddenly – you know how it comes, usually with some sudden happy thought – for no particular reason at all, I become very happy, and immediately my yellow robins come again, and go through all their circus. Coincidence perhaps, or are they trying to show me that they love me as much as I love them? I have lived among them for over twenty years, and they always come to me with their funny little antics in the moments of my greatest joy or sorrow.

Our playground was peopled with many small, grey lizards with dragonlike spikes from head to tail. They looked like miniature survivors of the dread reptilian age. When disturbed they ran up the nearest fence post and sat atop, snapping at us with vicious looking but fairly harmless, mustard-yellow mouths. Frequently these lizards, in trying to crawl through the wire netting fence, would become stuck with the frilly spikes entangled in the meshes of the wire; we used to go to some pains to release them, after which they showed their gratitude by chasing and attempting to bite us.

One day, a huge black snake disturbed the "quiet" of our lunch hour; Ped grabbed a willow stick and went to do battle, but the Joe Blake, as snakes were locally known, retreated under a pile of flood-drift beneath a great weeping willow. The drift was fired with much ceremony; Ped and Pat Cullen, the two senior boys of the school, stood on sentry duty armed with sticks almost as large as themselves, with which to kill the monster as he came out of the fire, but he stayed in and was killed and cremated in the one act. Our triumph took a sad turn, when it was found that the fire had also killed our lovely willow.

The feature of our daily lunch was the boiling of the tea Billy. Just before lunch Ped and Pat were sent out to make the fire; that was a simple task, dead eucalyptus leaves blaze like petroleum, then follow twigs, sticks and long rolls of brittle bark shed from the gum trees (the earlycomers to Australia found our gum trees to be a paradox in that they retained their leaves in the winter, but shed their bark). By the time school was disbanded for lunch time recess the Billy was boiling and every child, no matter how small, drank a pannikin of tea. Milk had been brought in a tomato sauce bottle and should the day be warm, the bottle was stood up to its neck in the water of the creek which gurgled under the shade of the willow tree.

Once during a drought, a horse belonging to Kanimbla Station most inconsiderately died in the marshy part of the creek a quarter of a mile above the school. It was one of those few patches which had given Long Swamp its name. The boundary rider had no chance of either burning the carcase or pulling it out of the quivering slime. We had been having "horse soup" for some days without knowing it, but when the awful truth became apparent, the teacher decreed that our drinking and tea water should come from Honeysuckle Creek which came into Long Swamp from a northern ridge some hundreds of yards downstream. Two little students, of whom I was nearly always one, were told off each day as water carriers. What fun it was; over half an hour of school time was allowed for the task.

Honeysuckle was a gentle little creek which trickled over pink granite, banked on either side by soft, delicately green Maidenhair fern, and was a spot beloved by Flame Robins. When Long Swamp was again proclaimed drinkable, we missed our little daily adventure, and longed (I even prayed) for another horse to come and die for us. On cold days when we had a merry fire roaring up our queer looking chimney, the lunch Billy was hung over the blaze, Heath Robinson fashion, on a series of loops and wires which in the first place had been taken from the boundary fence, most probably without permission.

The first lesson of the day was called Observation. We were required to write brief essays about any interesting natural phenomena or anything relating to natural history observed on the way to school; the subject was always of our own choosing. Two miles of varied bush track with many creek crossings, gave unlimited material for our young, greedy minds. I hope that Observation is still part of the curriculum of bush schools; it teaches children to discover Nature for themselves, and such intimacy with Nature's secrets nearly always leads to a strong desire to protect all beautiful and useful wild life. It leads, too, to the quiet philosophy of the true Nature lover, a priceless acquisition which enables one, no matter what the environment, to live apart and view as from a distance, the hurrying world; something which makes the voice of the grey thrush in your shrubs more desirable than the purr of a thousand guinea motor car in your garage; makes beetles more interesting than bonds, and sunsets more desirable than securities. I know now that the Observation lessons in that tiny thatched school were the lessons that did me the most good.

I shall be happy to remember always those neighbours who lived up the creek and with whom I studied, while the thrushes perched and sang on the window ledge and the goannas peeped in at the open door; with whom I played under the willows and sailed toy boats on the creek. These were my first friends, and are still my best friends.

Sometimes we had dances at our new home, and they were great fun; people came riding for many miles, and usually slept at our place afterwards – mostly on shakedowns. We had no piano, but the music of Herb's accordion was more stirring to me than the greatest of Sydney's dance orchestras is now. Yogi played the fiddle, and kept one foot tapping so the time would be right. A fiddle it was, and Yogi would not understand what you meant if you called it a violin. Yogi was a quiet, friendly, musical old aboriginal, and a whiter man than a great many chaps I've met since.

Many city people have the wrong impression about dancing in the country; there are no picture theatres, concerts, bridge parties or night tennis clubs in the outback country, so that dancing is the only form of public evening recreation, and though a country person's steps may not be quite as up to date as those of one living in the city, it is my considered opinion – having experienced both – that the average country resident is a better dancer than the average city dweller.

Somewhere about 1910 I remember getting up before dawn, and shivering in a funny little night-shirt thing, while I got my first glimpse of Halley's Comet lying horizontally above the eastern horizon, just as the stars were paling. It was a glorious sight. For many mornings I did this, until the comet, taking pity perhaps as it looked down upon my scanty attire, began to appear instead in the west, and at dusk. If there is any reason why I want to live to a great age, it is to see Halley's Comet again. Mother and Dad were disappointed with Halley's Comet, but then they had seen the monster which came unheralded and dominated the skies of 1884 – the greatest recorded comet in the history of the world.

Another day well remembered was the Coronation Day of the late King George the Fifth. It had rained the night before; then a stinging hard frost froze the raindrops on the grass and leaves. In the morning, the whole landscape – grass, trees, ferns, spiderwebs and wire fences – was hung with large dazzling ice diamonds, which threw back the rays of the wintry sun. My uncle, Bernard Carlon, the "Grand old man of Burragorang", after whom I was named, was with us and remarked that we on Long Swamp had, that morning, a finer display of jewels than Westminster Abbey would see that day.

About this time – at the age of six – I remember seeing my first train at Blackheath.

The years brought realisation that, with the rabbits lessening the grazing capacity for sheep, our land could no longer support such a large family as it had hitherto done. There was a council of war, and it was decided to sell the old home. The five brothers who were older than I would go to Queensland to cut out new homes from virgin country, and the rest of the family would settle temporarily in Megalong, a sunken valley west of Katoomba. This moving business was exciting, and

I just could not get started quickly enough, but now, when I look back, I know that those days in the old home were the happiest days my family knew. It was in that house that the whole family assembled for the last time under one roof, and though I was only seven years old when we left it, as I write I can still clearly see those summer nights of such a long time ago, out on the old verandah facing the east, with the great cream rambler rose trailing over one end and across the tank. Mother is just inside, darning socks or putting baby Joe to sleep, the light of her lamp streams out across the verandah, and lights up the big mulberry tree, in the branches of which the girls and I are trying to distinguish the black berries from the red ones. Norb, Mick and Ped are wrestling in the grass or jumping in the air to try to catch bats; many of these little chaps are flying about, and the beating of their velvet wings makes soft music in the still summer evening. Herb is sitting on the verandah edge with his legs dangling; he is playing his accordion. Tom is in a deck chair, playing his flute. Dad sits on the floor, his back against the verandah post and his legs sprawled, puffing away at his old pipe he had carved the bowl himself out of a briar root. A great yellow moon comes up over Marsden's Rock and paints the scene with shimmering silver. The scent of Dad's beloved lilacs is in the air; a willy wagtail pipes "pretty little creature!" from the acacia tree. Crickets sing in the long grass down beside the fence; a sheep bell tinkles in the distance, and the soft voice of a mopoke comes fitfully from the moonlit gums on Round Ridge. Perhaps some day in a place called Heaven we may be allowed to re-enact scenes like these.

At last, we set off for Megalong. Rose and I double-banked on a fat round pony named Silky, with a couple of fowls slung over in a chaff bag with holes cut for their heads. At Chapploe Creek and Five Mile Creek we stopped to put water on the chooks' heads, for they showed signs of overheating.

Megalong meant a strange school and new boy and girl friendships – firm friendships which also have lasted through the years. The house at Megalong, Glenwood, was very poor compared with our old one, but it was smothered in English honeysuckle vines, and the wee Spinebill honeyeaters were always with us. Our variety of Spinebill is, I believe, the only Australian representative of the humming bird family.

Our little spineys were wonderful acrobats, and frequently when alighting on a bunch of flowers, the vine would bend under their weight, until the birds hung vertically and upside down. Remaining in that position they would insert their little cobbler's awl bills into bloom after bloom, sipping out the honey until they were exhausted or satisfied to the point of discomfort. I have watched these birds by the hour, and have found that most of their meals are taken whilst standing on their heads.

Megalong is flanked by the great red and yellow ramparts of the Blue Mountains, but the greatest beauty of the valley lies in its wild flowers. Megalong Creek in Spring was a winding ribbon of gold, and then, when the wattle blooms had fallen and the myriad balls of golden fluff had drifted off down the creek, the red and pink bottle brushes and the white grevillias came out. Back on the sandstone benches grew every known variety of flowering heath, and in the big bush country nearby there was a species of wattle in bloom during every month of the year – every day was Wattle Day.

Back in the mountains towards Nellie's Glen were forests of waratahs, and one day up above a rocky ledge under Narrow Neck, I came upon an acre of flannel flowers in bloom.

A hundred yards from the house were sandstone caves where stone axes, flint scrapers and other aboriginal relics were to be found; these caves were peopled by saucy rock wallabies which in flight were fearless, agile creatures travelling at full speed round the face of a cliff where no human climber would dare to follow. Wild currants, red and black, Geebungs and Cherry Cypress, all shapely as any pruned shrubs, grew thickly over the rocky ridges. Each in season bore edible berries which provided young explorers with many an impromptu meal when far from home. The "puddens" of Long Swamp had been left far below but soon we found a tiny vine with an edible, roly-poly berry; this was at once named "Pudden Vine" and such is the fickle favour of youth, that the original "puddens" were pushed into the background and out of our memories. Blackberries of course were plentiful, but since they formed a part of the home menu in the role of pies and preserves, there could be no thrill in eating them when on an exploring trip. At that time small attention was paid to the encroaching blackberry menace; it was not until some years later that it was declared to be the worst plant pest in New South Wales.

Back beyond the skyline above the great cliffs was the clean, new, tourist town of Katoomba, proud hub of the famous Blue Mountain scenery; it was six miles away by a narrow bridle track and thither we went to be initiated to the mysteries of our first moving picture show. The miles of bush track left a more lasting impression than "The Pictures". First the way was through thick gum country with grass trees and sometimes a peep at the swift creek with its teatree and red bottlebrushes. Here and there were gaunt white stone chimneys, silent witnesses of the great bushfire. Though I was too young then to have any deep feelings about them, there was something silent and terrible about these mute relics of happy homes. A few years later I was, on one occasion, returning from Katoomba alone at night; my nerves were all on edge from the contemplation of a mythical tiger which had been "seen" more than once in the thick bush below Nellie's Glen (almost every rural district in New South Wales has had its "tiger" scare at some time or other). Travelling faster than necessary I rode suddenly into a clearing with a group of these chimneys. In the light of a small moon, the terror which went through me was as real as though I had seen the monster; the pony, perhaps infected by my fear, gave a great plunge and bolted through the big timber for home; at the house two miles away they heard the ring of his hooves on the hard, pipeclay road and the family waited anxiously at the garden gate while a terrified boy and an equally frightened animal came flying towards them through the night.

Beyond the chimneys, the track climbed sharply; gums and stringybarks gave way to lofty turpentines, sassafras, cedars, wattles, treeferns and waratahs. High above was Boar's Head, a thousand foot crag of yellow sandstone, capped by a grotesque looking head more suited to a dragon than to a boar. This was the beginning of Nellie's Glen, a narrow, awful crevice in the gigantic cliffs, through which the track zigzagged amongst hanging balconies of ferns and dripping spray of waterfalls. Down the glen even on the hottest days, rushed an icy draught, the breath of waterfalls and the pungent scent of sassafras. This, too, was the home of the southern Lyrebird whose classic beauty, glorious ringing call and incomparable mimicry have given it a unique position in the avian world. Above the Glen the character of the country changed again to stunted, colourful heath, boronia, dwarf banksias, trigger plants and mountain devils. Mountain devils are the joy of Blue Mountain children; following a tulip-shaped flower of flame-red comes the seed pod – a perfect little devil's head with two sharp horns and a sinister-looking, pointed beard. Equipped with gnarled twigs or pipestem cleaners to supply various limbs and tail, they make toys or grotesque little ornaments which are always in demand by tourists, as souvenirs.

Now that I look back it is a great source of wonder to me that, no matter how far afield our individual rambles and explorations took us, we were never reprimanded by Mother or Dad; their complete confidence in our ability to look after ourselves in strange, heavily timbered country was something that was taken for granted.

CHAPTER VI

Our Turn As Pioneers

WHILE we were settling down in our new home and living in a constant state of excitement as one by one the valley yielded its secrets, a different scene was being enacted in Queensland, some hundreds of miles north, in the Brisbane Lands Office. Eight long lean young men, all O'Reilly, were going through the formalities of selecting eight blocks of land high up in the centre of the uninhabited Mcpherson Range country which is now known as Lamington National Park. Three of the boys were our cousins Pat, Luke and Joe; the others were brothers Tom, Herb, Norb, Mick and Ped. Ped was a big overgrown boy just promoted to long trousers. An advance party of the boys had already been to inspect the land. The blocks were sprawled across the rugged top of a high volcanic plateau; the soil was bright red, deep and rich enough to support a lavish rain forest;

giant trees stood together thicker than the pillars in a cathedral with an undergrowth of tangled vine where every step had to be won by the chop of a brush hook. The plateau, like Conan Doyle's Lost World, was ringed by great cliffs and accessible only at one point by a bridle path over which only the hardiest of mountain horses could travel. The nearest vehicular road was sixteen miles distant; it was of bottomless black soil, trafficable only in dry weather. The nearest railway terminus was Beaudesert, twenty-six miles away.

One may now picture those young men standing in the twilight of that magnificent, terrible forest, measuring with their eyes those trees which would have to be cut down, burnt and cleared, before even one blade of grass would grow; measuring too their own hard muscles and thinking "Can we do it?" Thinking too of that sixteen miles of nightmare track up the range over which all the food, tools, blankets and equipment must be carried on their broad backs until there would be grass enough to support a packhorse. We know now that it was a task which should never have been attempted, that it was hard enough finally to break the spirit of those iron men, but we know just as surely that it was the very colossal nature of the task, which made it an irresistible challenge to young men whose veins ran rich with pioneering blood – men who were bred in difficult times and whose lives had been just a succession of obstacles to be overcome.

There was another factor; this new country, ruthless and terrible though it was, was the most magnificent they had yet seen. This to men familiar from boyhood with the Blue Mountains (then regarded as the scenic wonderland of Australia), meant that some day when Queensland began to appreciate her own worth their land would be in the heart of scenery which would challenge the world's best.

Could we but see a little way around the corner into the future, there are many things which we would not do. Our big boys did not see the cards which were to he stacked against them for more than a generation, so they signed up for their selections. Their faith in the future of Queensland and in their own powerful bodies was superior to all obstacles; they signed and became Queensland citizens.

Our cousins, Pat, Luke and Joe, had also taken up selections on the plateau and accompanied our boys on their great adventure.

Next day saw them rolling along a black soil road in a five-horse coach to Kerry Light-hearted and with the spirit of adventure running high they waved their straw hats to everybody, while their striped Broadway ties floated back in the breeze. It was a typical Queensland midwinter day, but what a joke midwinter can be in Queensland – warm, almost hot, sunshine and an indigo sky; the cultivation paddocks rich with green; bananas and tomatoes ripening on the hill side. Kerry was having its winter race meeting that day. The racecourse was at Shamrock Vale, the home of the pioneer Deerain family. The actual track which followed a wide bend of the Albert River is nine furlongs of dead level oval loam. Near the finishing post there is a deep, blue lagoon fringed with red bottlebrush trees, which lean over the water. The lagoon serves the double purpose of beautifying the racecourse and acting as a subtle threat to defaulting bookmakers.

After breakfast next morning, eight human packhorses were soon on their way, carrying their heavy loads towards Cainbable Gorge, a huge wooded gash which penetrates far back into the ranges, and up the bed of which the first few hours of going lay. From the head of the gorge, the track climbed a ridge, which might well have been called the Heartbreaker. It rose from the valley floor to the plateau two thousand feet above in one steep climb of less than a mile; after rain it was very dangerous, slippery as ice, and packhorses frequently slid twenty yards and more without taking their feet off the ground. From the rim of Cainbable cliffs above the Heartbreaker, unfolds one of the most extensive views in Australia. From east to west for over fifty miles stretch the Mcpherson Ranges and the Great Divide magnificent broken masses of dark blue, while to the north, gently undulating, is the vast coastal plain of south-east Queensland, stretching away as far as the Blackall Range, one hundred and thirty miles away. It has been said that this point overlooks an area equal to that of Tasmania.

There is an aboriginal legend woven about Cainbable Cliffs; it concerned a primitive murder and the story was told to us by the late John Horan, one of the Albert River pioneers. Years before white man came, a black warrior of the Moreton Bay tribe took unto himself a handsome young gin. Shortly after the ceremonies some organic trouble developed and she lost the sight of her eyes. This was bad enough in the tribal camp on the river flats, but when time for the winter walkabout came and the whiptail wallabies went far back into the ranges, imagine what a handicap she was. In a hunting party a gin's place was to follow behind the Spearsman, carrying babies, spare weapons, food and oddments of gear; the blind gin, far from being a help, was an encumbrance; her disgusted man had to lead her by the hand through the gorges and over the ridges. When they came to an obstacle, log or rock, he would say, "Yump", and she would jump it; should the obstruction be large the command was altered to, "Big fella yump", and the gin increased her leap accordingly. At length the walkabout led them to the Kangaroo Grass country on the top of Cainbable, and the warrior, through hindrance to his hunting and perhaps also because of the gibes of fellow spearsmen, finally reached the end of his patience with the poor blind gin. He led her all unsuspecting up to the brink of the great cliffs and said, "Big fella yump" and she did.

"And," the narrator concluded, "she went with a yaah."

On from the cliff walls a mile of tramping through Kangaroo grass along an undulating rocky ridge took the big boys to the edge of the jungle. The jungle begins as a green wall over a hundred feet high, as definite and almost as impenetrable as the ramparts of a medieval city. One moment you are walking through open country with stringybarks, sugargums and giant grass trees, these living links with forgotten ages; then with one step through the dark portals of the jungle you leave the sunshine behind and with it every semblance of vegetation through which you have been passing – every genus and every species, every bird and animal in that one step changes as drastically as if you had suddenly set foot on Mars. Here tower bright green soft woods smothered in all manner of living parasites, orchids and ferns; looped and twined with hundreds of feet of great vines, thick as the upper arm. The jungle teems with exotic birds who never cross the dark threshold into the sunny warmth of the eucalyptus country. Here, too, are colourful outlandish flowers which bloom only in the green twilight.

The first march of the young pioneers was over; the sixteen miles of rough uptrack had been traversed in a day, a job which would be hard to parallel now; the average load had been over a hundred pounds per man. Pat, Luke and Joe had stayed to camp on Pat's block of land; the five brothers went on to the first of their holdings, Herb's, where a lovely, jungle stream lined with banks of great lilies had reached the edge of the plateau and dashed itself to powdery spray into the green gorge below. Between the wall of timber and the cliff rim ran an open strip a few yards wide, a breathing space which was chosen for a camp site. Before blankets were rolled out, six tiger snakes had to be killed and two bulldog ants' nests burnt out. Herb had been sitting on the brink of the cliff watching the opalescent spray of the falls leaping out into the twilight. On getting up to go back to the camp site, he found two hissing flattened reptiles blocking his path; there was no stick handy and no retreat. "Bring a stick!" he yelled to the others. "Two snakes here!"

"You can have my stick," Norb called out, a bit out of breath, "as soon as I've finished killing these beggars over here." Two carpet snakes and a twelve foot rock python were spared – they proved useful about the camp later by eradicating bush rats. It would have been a bad camp for a sleepwalker; three yards from the foot of their leafy beds was certain death over the three hundred feet cliffs; behind their heads was a tangled mass of thorn, stinging tree and burning vine, which the jungle always uses as a first line of defence; over in the coarse tussocks beyond the campfire lived a large community of tiger snakes and death adders, which for centuries had been lords of this one, sunbaked ledge on the vast, gloomy plateau. Such trifles do not trouble men who carry a horse's pack all day, and so, undisturbed by the howling of dingoes and the scream of Powerful Owls, the first night passed in heavy sleep.

So many necessities had to be brought on the first long carry that a tent was ruled out as a luxury. Early next morning the ancient cliffs which had brooded over the changes of countless centuries were echoing with a new sound; that sound which more than any other symbolises the conquest of Australia – the ring of the settler's axe. A little bark bumpy was being built. Tom and Herb were cutting, dressing and carrying long poles for the framework; Ped was levelling on a site at the brink of the falls, while Norb and Mick stripped big sheets of bark from convenient stringybarks and tallowwoods. These sheets were about eight feet by three; when stripped they were laid flat on the ground, and weighted down with rocks to prevent curling. When dry enough they were nailed to the pole frame with a weatherproof overlap, and so the bumpy was completed. The stripping of bark is fairly easy in winter when the sap is up, but at any other time of the year, it is almost impossible.

In earlier generations a bark bumpy formed the nucleus of the homes of thousands of Australian selectors, serving the settlers during the first bad days until time and money permitted of a more comfortable dwelling, this time a solid slab house with a shingle roof or a galvanised iron roof if possible. The bumpy would then do duty as a cart shed and harness room. Later still when a little hard-won prosperity had come the selector's way, a fine new house would be built of Caun timber with a corrugated iron roof. The slab house would then be used as a kitchen and rooms for hired help. It would be connected to the new house by a kind of platform; at this stage the old bark building, usually passed on to its Valhalla and became just one of the many memories of the early bad times. Such was the genesis of the selector's home in the early days.

With their few household goods now secured against the weather, our boys sharpened axes and brush hooks for their assault on the timber. First hooks were used to slash the thorny, stinging entanglements which defied entry to the great forest: the whole area to be felled was then thoroughly cleared of all underbrush so that there would be room for the free swinging of axes. This done, the more serious phase of the work commenced; for months the great gorges thundered with the sound of falling giants; not since the grim morning of the world when volcanic might had built it, had such a cannonading been heard on the plateau.

The felling of jungle at that time was considered to be the most dangerous work in Queensland, carrying as it did the highest insurance premium under the Workers' Compensation Act. To men unfamiliar with the work it was doubly dangerous. It was Pat who in later years said, "Our guardian angels were working overtime." Three factors contribute largely to the danger. First the majority of jungle trees have no tap roots, they are supported mainly by high buttresses which in many cases extend more than twelve feet from the tree proper, and which make treefelling from the ground level an impossibility. This calls for the use of a springboard; made of light wood, four feet long and a foot wide, it has at one end a steel tip, which is inserted into a horizontal slot cut into the tree. Toe holes are cut up the tree to the required height, the board is fixed and then on this narrow rocking perch, the settler swings his razor-edged axe, sometimes twenty and even thirty feet from the ground, which bristles with the sharp stumps of slashed undergrowth. Then, when the tree begins to go, he must descend swiftly, bringing not only his axe but his springboard – all good fellers bring their boards to the ground to obviate the possibility of fouling by the falling tree.

The second danger lies in the extremely treacherous nature of the free-grained, brittle, soft woods which predominate; the very structure of these trees, eighty or more feet of limbless bole and a heavy umbrella top, accentuates this danger.

The swaying of the heavy tops may form wind cracks right up through the heart of the tree. Suppose – and here I quote a case which is not infrequent – a man on a springboard fifteen feet from the ground has just chopped into the heart of a tree: a puff of wind bends the heavy top outwards, then with the sound of a bursting bomb, the trunk splits up through the heart as far as the branches; the riven half lashes out and upwards, perhaps sixty feet with a fearful sweep, as the head drops forward; for a split second the tree may balance horizontally by the middle on the shattered, upright trunk sixty feet above, then, pivoting wildly, it drops full length beside the stump. From first to last, the calamity may have taken three seconds or less; even had there been time for action, no one could predict the ultimate position of that one hundred and fifty feet of tree as it struck the ground; human action is powerless, the axeman is in the hands of God.

There are other contingencies, faulty grain or well-concealed hollows or dry rot, which may upset a man's calculations and send a tree suddenly back over him; he may have time to jump, but no time to pray.

One day early in 1913, Herb was chopping twenty feet up on a great leaning Litsea tree. It was apparently sound but as proved later, had a large hollow; the narrow timber outside of the hollow which was carrying the whole strain must have been as taut as a violin string, for after twenty minutes chopping, the whole side of the tree literally exploded without warning. Herb jumped from his board, round to the side of the tree and hung by his hands from the cut while the monster ripped to pieces around him. He was unharmed, but his shattered spring hoard was found twenty-two yards away and his axe buried under tons of debris.

At any of the great National Shows of Australia, you may witness splendid exhibitions of skill and daring by champion axemen on high spring boards, but these, hair-raising as they may be, are but child's play compared with the real thing. Instead of turf below, the settler has rocks and murderous spikes; instead of a light block above the cut, a hundred tons of quivering destruction tower above him; instead of cheering thousands, he has one spectator, the grim figure of Death forever at his elbow.

We come now to the third great danger in felling; it arises from the long, tough ropes of watervine with which the whole jungle roof is interwoven, making a bridge from one tree to another. A big tree in falling, may, through the medium of these vines, tear off large portions of a treetop fifty yards behind it, in the direction in which an axeman is most likely to run for cover; again a big vine, well anchored behind, may by its pull, deflect the falling tree into a high fork from which it will slide back off its own greasy stump and bury its butt in the earth a chain away.

In the felling of rain forest, much chopping may be saved, especially in hilly country, by the use of the "drive" system. This, roughly, is the cutting of say half an acre of trees only two thirds of the way through and then "sending them off", with a big drive tree dropped from the uphill side; the pressure goes on slowly at first and then gains momentum, as each tree is pushed from behind and in turn pushes the one in front; the big water-vines too, play an important part. The trees do not break off level at the cut; they rip and burst under the pressure, and it is, a terrifying sight to see a large strip of lofty forest tearing itself to pieces to the accompaniment of sounds which cannot be described. Driving is a science which is not learned in a day or in a season. Every tree must have its cut faced so that when the pressure comes on, it will fall on the one ahead; often this sequence is followed in a semicircle to hit straggling trees at right angles from the general direction of the drive. In sawing down a tree it is always possible with the aid of lifting wedges, to drop it within inches of an objective, but in axe work, with its large margin of error, each separate tree presents its own problem in lean and stress.

Sometimes a drive may become hung halfway through, owing to the stubborn resistance of some tough tree. It is possible to release it by going in to chop the hang-up tree until it gives away, but the chances of getting out again are not bright. To go in under a thousand tons of crackling, groaning timber and chop until it is almost ready to grind you to pulp, is perhaps the most foolhardy act one could conceive, though I should be the last to say so, because more than one of my brothers have been guilty of such folly. Left alone, the silent pressure will finally do its work on a hung-up drive, usually in the small hours when the sounds are made even more terrible by the hush of night. Tom, who notices such things, says that on a still night a drive will always go with the beginning of ebb tide at the nearest ocean beach, the tidal drag gives extra pressure needed to set the drive in motion. Through long observation he has always found this to be the case.

The chief danger in driving is that the drive tree may skid back off its own stump after striking the tree in front. In 1913, Norb and Tom had a narrow escape in these circumstances. Norb was felling his drive tree from a high board and at a seemingly safe distance of over twenty yards back up the hill, Tom was chopping into a big Mariara tree high above the ground. As Norb's tree commenced to go, he came to earth and ran back up the hill for safety. The tree, a long straight Booyong, fell squarely into the fork of the next tree, its heavy top snapped off, and all in an instant the trunk was skidding back down out of the fork, across its own high stump and shot like a giant spinning arrow for Tom's springboard. Norb's long leg took him in a great sideways leap out of the line, but he felt its wind on the back of his neck. Tom jumped from his board and hung to the cut on the far side of the tree. The distance from Norb's to Tom's tree measured afterwards was almost seventy feet.

There are many instances (far too many), which I could quote of those first three years, when death or serious injury passed close to our boys. Injury, however, did not always pass by; slippery springboards on damp days and high climbing with keen axes presented so many opportunities for accident that on the law of average something had to happen. Ped was the first; a leg gash with a severed tendon took him to Beaudesert hospital for over two months. While the other boys were away earning money for further improvements, Norb, working alone on the selections, cut his leg badly. Unable to catch a horse and go for treatment, he had recourse to his own surgery; ten stitches were put in the wound with the only sewing materials in the humpy, a rusty sewing needle and black cotton. Mick fell from a springboard and was impaled on a spike; he was taken the long slow journey to hospital in terrible agony; a good recovery was made and he suffered no permanent effect. On another occasion, both Herb and Pat went to hospital on the same day suffering from axe cuts. Herb's was a cut tendon which is still noticeable; Pat's gash was on the lower abdomen, a little more and it could have killed him; as it was, loss of blood was his most serious trouble.

Tom, though he carries no scars of those early days, had perhaps the most painful mishap of all. He was working, stripped to the waist as our axemen always worked, on a small Gympie tree, when it twisted in a choppy wind and fell across him, burying his half-naked body in its huge stinging leaves. The other boys cut strips of bark from the trunk of the Gympie and rubbed the inside with its slimy sap over Tom's skin until he got some measure of relief.

The Gympie stinging tree, or Gympie Gympie, as it is called by the blacks, is readily identified by its huge dinner-plate leaves a foot across. The leaves and young stems are hairy with transparent, stinging spines and contact with them is as painful as a scald with boiling water; the agony is not confined to the injured spot; it is just as intense in the underarm, neck and groin glands, which also swell noticeably. The most popular antidote is the juice of a beautiful calla lily, the cunjevoi which, strangely enough, always grows around the foot of the Gympie; our boys, however, established that the "tail of the dog that bit you" – the sap of the tree itself, is far superior. The invisible sting barb which is embedded in the skin of the victim, is a tiny funnel filled with venom, so that for many days after the first agony has abated, if the injured part is dipped into water, more poison will be forced

Pat's Bluff

Top: The Stinson; Above: Part of Proud's "diary"

The plane
wreckage

Above: Bernard O'Reilly,
having a well-deserved rest

Opposite:
Top: The rescue; Bottom: Joe Binstead

Peter O'Reilly

Jane O'Reilly

Top: Burragorang Valley
Above: Head of Kanangra Gorge

This page Top: Pat's bark humpy 1912. The first building on the plateau, on the brink of Raining Cliff. Pat (left) and Joe. Above: The humpy on Moran's Creek, 1912. From the left: Mick, Ped, and Norb. On the right, Luke.

Opposite page: Top: The first lady visitors to the plateau. Centre: New beginning – first section of the guest house. Bottom: Saw pit and mill (Herb using the pit saw).

This page:
Above: The first hut.
Below: At the guesthouse.

Opposite page:
A Giant Water Vine

This page:
Clockwise from top:
Ann, Rose and Molly

Opposite page:
*Sarcochilus
hartmannii*

Gwongurai Falls, Toolona Creek

Antarctic Beech, showing depth of erosion over the centuries.

"Nature! great Parent! whose directing Hand
Rolls round the Seasons of the changeful Year,
How mighty! how majestick are thy Works!"
James Thomson, Winter – A Poem, 1726

The author – Bernard O'Reilly

through the small end of the funnels into the flesh, and thus the pain may be restarted at any time up to a fortnight.

People who work amongst them often make minor contact with the leaves, and constant stinging gives a certain amount of immunity. This had been so with Tom – had it not been, his case would probably have been fatal. There have been some recorded deaths in North Queensland from Gympie stings, in fact its record is worse than that of the universally feared black snake. These trees are plentiful on the lower part of the plateau, but are almost non-existent above three thousand feet. Next to the giant Tristanias, Gympies are the largest trees of Green Mountains; a girth of forty feet is not uncommon. In the lower gorges there is yet another stinger, a small tree with glossy leaves like a hydrangea, which inflicts a very painful sting. After the rainy season these leaves lose most of their barbs, so that during the winter they are fairly harmless. There is a small insect which lives exclusively on Gympie leaves, devouring them stings and all; we don't know his name, but we call him the He-man beetle; he seems to have found the ideal formula for hot meals at all hours.

❧

In writing of the hazards of timber felling, I have digressed. We shall now return to those first days of the humpy by the cliff. As may be supposed, the larder was limited to foods which would keep indefinitely; the sole diet in that first year was corned beef, damper, potatoes, onions, golden syrup, tea, sugar and salt.

In fact, with the sole addition of garden vegetables, this was the plateau diet for six years; towards the end of the Great War, milk and butter were added and later still we sometimes had fresh beef. Golden syrup was chosen in preference to jam because of its higher food value, and also because the empty tins were useful as billy cans. If the deadly monotony made the next meal a disagreeable prospect, then the next meal was postponed until it became a pleasant one.

Only once in that first year was the fare varied. A piece of corned beef had been left soaking in running water on top of the falls; by this process much of the salt was removed and stews were made possible. Mick on going down with a lantern to get the beef one night found a large eel feeding off it. Mr. Eel was dazed by the lantern light and was an easy target for a stick; he passed on to the frying pan with a hearty vote of thanks. As it is a well known fact that eels spawn in ocean depths, their appearance in a creek above three hundred feet of beetling cliff is hard to explain, even allowing for their known ability to travel overland. That first eel was not an isolated case; they proved to be very common and elvers (young eels) four inches long have been seen above the falls. Here is another eel problem for the experts. Some years ago workmen were giving a periodical cleanout to a pressure tank on top of the Hotel Carrington in Katoomba. The tank was some thirty feet from the ground. An eel many times larger than the inlet pipe was found there.

Since kerosene was too great a luxury for the

weekly carry from Kerry, the evening meal was always eaten by firelight. All the Billy cans looked alike in the uncertain light so that when a chap dived his hand into a Billy to get another potato, he sometimes inadvertently stuck it into hot tea or stew. In order that the day would not be started on cold corned junk, a stew was usually left to simmer above the coals all night. One morning it was found that all of the meat was missing from the stew; a watch was kept next night and the culprit proved to be a brush tail water rat almost double the size of a guinea pig. This rat is sometimes called the Beaver rat because of his aquatic habits. On another occasion the stew instead of being depleted was added to; a sandshoe which had been hung on a hook to dry above the fire was found in the stew next morning. It was at the end of the week and provisions were so scarce that despite the unusual ingredient the stew was eaten with relish.

Since it was part of the terms of selection that substantial improvements had to be effected within twelve months, certain acreage of jungle was cleared on each of the five blocks of land. By the time this had been done money was running short. It was decided to leave the Plateau temporarily and earn money for further development. Some of the boys took jobs as pine fellers with Lahey's Limited, then the largest sawmilling organisation in Queensland whose huge sawmill at Canungra was one of the seven wonders of the State. The Lahey brothers were far-seeing men who secured huge tracts of jungle, rich in pine, extending far up every gorge and plateau in the north-eastern part of the Mcpherson Range. At the time the boys went to work for them a great army of men was cutting timber high up in the beautiful Coomera Gorge. The great pine trees were felled and barked, the downhill ends were then given a sharp nose so that they would glance off obstacles. Finally, with the aid of wallaby jacks they were set in motion and shot like meteors to the bottom of the gorge, half a mile below; it was spectacular work and interesting.

Others of the boys came back to jobs on the Blue Mountains, and so by October, 1912, we had them all back in Megalong Valley. They told of jungles and palm trees, and orchids, and the Regent bowerbirds, and mound-building turkeys, and Birds of Paradise. But no mention was made of facts, which we were to learn afterwards, that the cutting down of the jungle is not only one of the hardest of tasks, but also the most dangerous in Australia; that there was no grass for the horses, and that all the food and implements had to be carried on the backs of those same big boys for sixteen miles – a little round trip of thirty-two miles. From the arrival of their first letters, the plateau had become the Promised Land to us – where we would all go when a home was cut out of the jungle.

Before leaving the plateau, Norb, having in mind Dad's interest in trees, spent some time cutting specimens of every variety of timber to take home. They were split into neat blocks four inches by two, each with its bark along the back. Being green timber, they were a big load on that sixteen mile walk down to Kerry. All were new to Dad; he handled them as reverently as if they had been holy relics, and exhibited them with pride to neighbours and callers in the years that followed.

Their names which we tried to memorise had a fine sound to us, "Silky oak, booyong, saffron heart, black myrtle, pencil cedar, rose mahogany". Once when Dad had brought his precious samples out to show relatives, a girl cousin catching sight of the blocks of wood gushed, "Oh, what have you got there, Uncle Peter – skittles?" Dad was disgusted.

Early in summer, 1912, Herb returned to the plateau, to fire the clearings and plant grass seed. The burning of felled, jungle is a splendid spectacle. You have perhaps a hundred or more acres covered to a depth of twenty feet with smashed timber and dry, leaves. A torch is made for firing, a stick with one flat end, bound around with kerosene soaked hessian with an outer binding of water soaked hessian to ensure steady burning. The torch is applied along the foot of the clearing, and flames, advancing in a wall, rush up the slopes with a roar which may be heard for many miles. Black smoke, boiling fiercely, shoots up to one thousand feet and there the terrible heat, contacting the icy upper air, generates a giant thunder cloud which rides majestically above the inferno. Only a volcano in full eruption can depict a scene as fiercely splendid as a big scrub fire. Sometimes the flames leaping far ahead, will span a small deep valley choked with debris dry as tinder. This, under the searing heat, gives off inflammable gas, until the valley is filled with some cubic acres of it, then it ignites with an explosion which tosses burning logs like twigs. To this is added the steady boom of exploding rock, which goes on for many hours after the fiercest of the blaze has subsided.

Grass seed, usually paspalum, must be planted

as soon as possible after the fire, so that it will sink into the soft ashes. Should rain fall before the planting, the ashes will set with a hard surface, and seed lying on top of it has a poor chance of striking. The planting is therefore done while the new clearing is still obscured by the bitter smoke of slow burning logs, and while the deep, downy ash is treacherous with beds of submerged coal.

Of all the selection work, that of planting – though not so hard – is the most painful. Once, years later, while I was planting from the top of a high log that the seed might scatter more widely, the still burning log began to roll; I jumped for safety but put my hand and all of my weight on a searing mass of white hot coal – someone else finished the planting.

So rich is the soil in mulch and potash that after the first fire good crops of corn, pumpkins or tomatoes may be had with no more extensive cultivation than a hole poked in the ashes with a sharp stick. Herb planted corn and paspalum, so that in a few months, with a small supply of feed assured, he bought a packhorse. It was shortly after the Presidential elections in the United States of America so the horse was named after Woodrow Wilson who had just then succeeded William H. Taft.

Pat, by this time, also had some grass so on the return trip from his old home he brought his horse, Dusty Bill. Dusty Bill had won many a ribbon in hurdle events in Blue Mountains Shows. On the boat trip from Sydney he kept in practice by jumping the high walls of his box and running loose on the deck of the *Wyarldra*. He scattered passengers and deck chairs like chickens and was just contemplating a jump over the deck rail in the direction of New Zealand when two stout seamen put an end to his mutiny.

To Dusty Bill and Woodrow Wilson fell the heroic task of packing the galvanized roofing iron for the six new slab humpies which were erected as improvements on the various blocks of land. To the farthest selection, Norb's, the pack was almost twenty miles; only a person who has transported galvanized iron by packhorse can appreciate the extreme difficulty to horse and man which that long pack through heavy timber represented. Dusty Bill, more because of his reputation as a "character" than because of his stout deeds, became a great favourite in the district and there was deep regret when he lost his life years later over the edge of a cliff on the Stockyard Creek track – a fate which he has shared with four other packhorses.

The first spoils of the new land were Ponderosa tomatoes weighing up to pounds each, pumpkins which would not fit into a corn sack, enough maize to serve Woodrow Wilson as hard feed for winter and enough paspalum to do him throughout the year. This first paspalum crop, partly supported by soft wood logs which had resisted the fire, reached in places a height of fourteen feet. Herb had also planted cabbage and lettuce, but few survived the ravages of the paddymelons, bandicoots and ringtails. Paddymelon is our smallest and most plentiful wallaby; the paradoxical name is a corruption of his aboriginal name "Paddi mella". All three marsupials swarm over the plateau. This is astounding in a country so thick with their natural enemies, the pythons, the dingo, the wedgetail eagle and the powerful owl.

The reaction of the birds to the felling of timber is worthy of note. One might easily imagine that the constant thunder of the falling forest would have the effect of scaring away all the birds in the locality; actually with a few exceptions, the position is reversed. The falling trees gouge out the earth and provide limitless food for ground birds; the smashing of the timber exposes undreamed of supplies of borers and grubs. The sap of trees and vines which exudes from the cuts and breaks, is the favourite food of many of our beetles and bugs – they come like the plagues of Egypt and with them come the insectivorous birds, literally in flocks. Instead of frightening them the clearing operations attract most of the birds for square miles around; the crash of a falling tree is a natural sound which does not alarm them; by contrast the report of a rifle, a lesser sound, will put to flight every bird within hearing.

Those staunch bushman's friends, the grey thrushes, followed our lunch fires for months during a felling job and existed almost entirely on the meat and bread we gave them and which they paid for, Tommy Tucker fashion, with their songs – there is a good reason why science has named our grey thrush, Harmonica. The meat we gave them was always salty and after lunch it was the usual thing to see a thrush perched on the edge of our water Billy, having a drink. Yellow robins and brown mountain thrushes will follow road or track making operations for many miles through the jungle and will fly down to take grubs and worms almost off the shovels of the workmen. Lyre birds and turkeys, too, find newly turned earth to be good scratching and feeding grounds.

This popularity of the coming of civilisation did not end when a clearing was burnt. The inkweed, cape gooseberry and raspberry crops which followed the fire attracted birds from the surrounding country; in the new clearings too, the breeding of insects ran riot, providing abundant food; the paspalum and Rhodes grass seed attracted many varieties of parrots both from the jungle and the eucalyptus country. It would be safe to say that, since the coming of the O'Reillys to Green Mountains, most of the birds – all pigeons, satin and regent bower birds, currawongs, all parrots, thrushes, cuckoos, golden whistlers, yellow robins, all flycatchers, wrens and small insect and fruit eating birds have increased in numbers at least one hundred per cent, directly as the result of the clearings and the free-fruiting second growth trees which surround them. All of this gives me to think that the early givers of our land laws lost a splendid opportunity of making provision whereby the settlers and the wild life could live amicably together to their mutual advantage. The vanishing of many of Queensland's valuable birds has been due not so much to the indiscriminate shooting as to the complete destruction of the timber which provided natural habitats and gave them shelter from their natural enemies. If a belt of natural timber varying from one to five chains wide, according to the area and location of the property, had been left around the boundary line of every holding in Queensland our feathered allies would still have been with us. Such things as grasshopper and caterpillar plagues would be non-existent; the dread blowfly scourge of the west would be curbed; the cane grub eradicated. The State would be a vast checkerboard of virgin timber and this new and urgent erosion problem could never have reached its present proportions. Another important factor is that added millions of green trees would materially assist towards the stabilisation of our rainfall.

It is too late now to talk about what might have been done, but it is not too late to do something. The situation must be faced some day and sacrifices must be made. We have only to look to those cradles of civilisation, Northern Africa and Syria, and their great areas of shifting sand, to find what happens to land when we take all and give nothing. The United States of America is now spending millions of dollars on a vast forest scheme to reclaim great areas of her rich, western empire which erosion has converted into a desert within the last twenty years. I have made no mention here of destructive birds but they can always be coped with; besides, when we weigh up the good with the bad is it not better to lose a few bushels of grain to the birds than to lose the whole crop to grasshoppers? There has always been a tendency to exaggerate damage by birds. I cannot help thinking here of the many thousands of emus which were destroyed for the good reason that they were supposed to spread prickly pear: later it was scientifically proved that prickly pear seed digested by emus was infertile. I am reminded here of a western man talking loudly of emus – "No fence will keep 'em out, they go over it like birds."

The new humpies, though they added a homelike touch to each clearing, were built primarily to comply with selection conditions. Unless there was some special job to do on a far selection, the boys generally lived together in the main building on Moran's Creek. This was built plumb on the boundary line which divided Herb's land from Ped's, and as half of it extended into each, it fulfilled the building conditions on both blocks of land. Similarly Pat and Luke built and lived in a fine roomy humpy which straddled the boundary line between their land. This trick of making one house fulfil the building conditions of two blocks of land was a common practice throughout Queensland wherever two brothers had adjoining selections. It was an arrangement well suited to the early days, but often led to serious trouble when one brother brought home a wife.

The selection work of those first years was not confined merely to the felling of new clearings. At first our boys thought that when the timber was fired and the grass sown the job was finished; they were to find that it was little more than beginning. The land was still choked with large softwood logs which are difficult to burn and which had to be cross burned and rolled together with levers before a beast could walk across it. Then, swift in the wake of a new grass came the dreaded fireweeds, tobacco, ink-weed and lantana. Lantana, in common with other of our major plant pests, was introduced into Australia as a garden shrub. Running wild in the subtropical climate, it took possession of hundreds of thousands of acres of the richest coastal land, until its evil reputation in Queensland was second only to that of another garden importation, the prickly pear, which overran one hundred thousand square miles of our best pastoral country. Like prickly pear, lantana is now combated by an imported insect. Any old selector will tell you that he would rather tackle clean standing jungle than a clearing overgrown with tobacco and lantana. The fireweeds were not all one-sided, however; two of the most common were cape gooseberry and cherry tomato, both welcome additions to the meal table.

Quite aside from the interloping fireweeds there is always the jungle itself, which never gives up its battle to reclaim a clearing. Almost as soon as the grass appears, roots, suckers and seedlings of nearly every jungle plant and vine, push up their heads like Phoenix from the ashes, so that in the first few years the brush hook cannot be allowed to remain idle long. It will be seen that the battle to win a grass clearing is not nearly so great as the battle to hold it. Then, in the midst of this struggle, money runs short; to accumulate more the selector goes away to work six months for someone else, and in doing so, runs not only the risk of losing his clearing through weed and second growth, but also of losing his selection by forfeit. Mick used to say that all of this came under the heading of "settling men on the land".

Apart from the second growth, the great walls of jungle which surround the clearing like green cliffs, never cease to encroach upon the land. The jungle is a greedy monster, but it does not rush to devour in the manner of monsters. It moves stealthily night and day; moves with a scientific procedure as carefully thought out as the campaign plan of a disciplined army. First a screen or barrage is thrown out, a network fifteen feet deep of thorny vine – raspberry, wait-a-while, nettle and burning vine, together with vicious hedges of gympie and bristling gin's whisker. This, the first line of offence impenetrable alike to man and beast, gives full protection to a forest of swift growing trees, mainly panax, duboisia, and melecope, which shoot up twenty-five feet in five years, and establish a new timber line. These trees are short lived, and only act as "pot boilers" while the slow growing permanent trees of the jungle are becoming established. Could any battle plan be more perfect? First is the curtain barrage, then, under its cover the shock troops advance and take position, holding it only until the regulars dig in and make it impregnable. All this time the barrage is going forward, and so the jungle advances with military precision, and as relentlessly as the march of time itself.

After the first hard years there was enough grass on the plateau for extra horses. Each brother then bought a saddle horse for himself; the days of the sixteen mile walk from Kerry passed for ever. In those few years before the Great War little more than two thirds of the time was spent on the selections; the rest of the time money was being earned to keep things going. Money too, was frequently sent back to Megalong Valley, for

Glenwood was not productive; Dad's mail contract, Molly's school, Mother's tiny post office and the skins of odd foxes and rabbits which we children trapped were the only sources of revenue.

On the plateau a new position now arose. Mr. Romeo Lahey, a member of the famous sawmilling family instigated a strong campaign for a national scenic reserve in the Mcpherson Ranges. This idea had been conceived in the previous century by the late Mr. Robert Collins, a well-known Logan River pastoralist. Mr. Collins was a man with vision far ahead of his time; he alone could see that Queensland would need this great scenic area, and he, alone of his day, battled to keep the area intact, but his vision was far ahead of the Lands Administration of the time, and he died without seeing the fulfilment of his dream.

When Mr. Lahey took up the cause, the position was perhaps more favourable to the idea. Queensland, after an orgy of destruction, had reached a stage where it could well begin to think of conservation. However that may have been, it is true that Mr. Lahey's vigorous championing of the cause, though it did not bear immediate fruit, finally moved the Government and resulted in the gazetting of the area. Queensland owes a large debt of gratitude to the late Robert Collins who conceived this splendid dream, to Romeo Lahey who carried it through to its fulfilment, and to the late Honourable J. M. Hunter, Minister for Lands, whose official act preserved for all time the glory of Lamington National Park.

It was in 1912 that the first shots were fired in Lahey's campaign, but the Government, averse to taking hurried action, shelved the matter for some years. Pending a decision, all the Crown land in the area was withdrawn from selection; thus the prospect of a group settlement on Green Mountains Plateau faded, and with it faded all immediate prospect of a road. Those were anxious years for the boys; there was much talk at first of the resumption of their land as an addition to the proposed park area, and at one time when the eight selectors were felling jungle, they were asked to desist, pending an offer to buy them out. Their axes lay idle for two months but no offer was made, either then or subsequently, so they went back to work and wrote off the loss of two months as experience.

The thought of resumption was a bitter one. There were few Australian settlers who had sufficient faith in the future of their properties to "back pack" their goods and gear sixteen miles, and there were few properties which would warrant such faith. The worst of the foot slogging had been done, human miracles had been worked. Green Mountains was not just a place where men took up land it was a dream which had led men to do superhuman tasks; it was a drug which had driven them like galley slaves; it was a Mountain Kingdom to be conquered, one which the difficulties and hardships had made even more desirable. Had the properties been resumed, it is probable that fairly adequate compensation would have been paid but what amount of money could compensate for the loss of that hope which had stimulated those first pioneering years?

For many years, the subtle threat of resumption hung over the properties like a dead leaning tree always ready to fall. Could any position be more disheartening? It was with anxiety and indecision that the work was carried on. Though Green Mountains was situated in the exact geographical centre of the proposed park it is still a source of wonder that the question of resumption should ever have arisen. The total area of the properties, less than one thousand acres, was very insignificant compared with the park area, more than 48,000 acres. Insignificant too compared with the huge tracts of rich jungle land held by timber interests and which abutted the park on every plateau and gorge, all of which would be despoiled by the pinefeller's axe. Why would the few acres of the struggling selectors be more desirable than the broad acres of the wealthy timber companies?

With the question of the park and road shelved indefinitely, the big boys began to look about for some easier means of access. With some scouting, done mostly on Sundays, they found that a way could possibly be made down into Stockyard Creek Gorge and hence out to Kerry. This route would shorten the trip to Kerry by five miles and the distance to the nearest waggon road by eight miles; also it eliminated the Heartbreaker. Ways and means had then to be considered. The first part would have to be blasted out of the face of a volcanic cliff for half a mile; from there a well-graded track would wind down the steep, grassy slopes to the floor of the Stockyard Creek gorge. After much argument and neck-breaking exploration the route was decided upon. The Beaudesert Shire Council agreed to supply tools and explosives. A small forge and anvil were packed up: these were for sharpening the steel drills. The packhorses caused many anxious moments by bumping cases of explosives against trees, but all arrived safely and the stage was set for the job.

The story of the building of Stockyard Creek Track does not rightly belong to this book; it is a story all of its own. It is a story of how the boys clung like flies as they drilled holes in the face of the cliff; how they fired their charges and climbed back behind a jutting angle of rock, hanging on like grim death while the cliff shook as from earthquake, and tons of rock avalanched into the valley, cutting off gum trees as though they were stalks of grass. For months the cannonade went on and every man, woman and child in the Logan and Albert River districts paused in their tasks to listen, and to remark that the mad men were at it again.

At last it was finished, even to the graded track down to the valley floor. A substantial rock wall, erected along the track edge on the cliff face, made it safe for riding, but it was as hair-raising as many a famous, old-world, mountain pass. The opening of the track was an occasion for rejoicing in the district. Riding parties, fifty strong, would trail up on Sundays, returning with extravagant tales of the scenery and the "supermen" who had conquered the cliff-walled stronghold and were holding it as did the knights of old by the strength of their arms.

With one of these early riding parties came our first visit from a press man; he was Teddy Bligh of the Beaudesert Times, and the truths he published in a subsequent full page article, stirred the district into action. Once more the matter was aired in the Shire Council's Chamber, once more the Government was approached, and once more the matter was dropped. Teddy Bligh answered the 1914 Roll Call, and like many another Logan and Albert boy, he lies in a bit of France which will be always Queensland.

CHAPTER VII

The Onward March

BACK in Megalong Valley things had been following their even course; the school, the swimming holes, bush rambles and the setting of rabbit traps, alternated in a manner which never permitted of monotony; always, too, in the rosy future was Queensland and the plateau, a wonderland built up on a thousand tales we had heard, and garnished by our own lavish imaginations; a future paradise which not one of us would have traded for eternal salvation. Living more in the future than in the present, we went on until August, 1914. I was the first at home to see it in the *Lithgow Mercury*, "Austria declares war"; I read it as "Australia" instead of "Austria", and the family rushed to see what it was about; then I came in for a lot of chaffing about not being able to spell.

The first few months were all glory and no horror for us. The sinking of the *Emden*; how we got worked up over that, and no wonder! Then there was the landing at Gallipoli – that was all glory too, but the war began to get nearer to us when a boy friend of ours was killed at Lone Pine.

Well I remember the fetes and bazaars and money drives for the Red Cross, the Comforts Fund, the Belgian Relief Fund, "Remember Belgium!" Who remembers now? Those little flags, red, yellow and black, which we stuck in our buttonholes – where have they gone? I remember the campaigns for conscription and the local bitterness which turned neighbour against neighbour – how some people would not deal with a certain tradesman because he had voted "Yes", or others who would not deal from another because he was a confessed "No" man! It all seems so stupid, and so futile, now. I remember work being suspended at our little school when the paper arrived with the news of the Battle of Jutland.

The War brought added hardship; there had been little enough money for necessities before, but with prices rocketing from fifty to a hundred per cent we went much of the time without meat and butter. Mother made all our clothes from cheap materials; she even kept the white calico flour and oatmeal bags, and after ripping open their seams and boiling out their trade lettering, made them up into shirts and underclothes for us. Boots and shoes were of course out of the question. Sometimes we had a cow and there would be milk for a while, but usually it finished by the cow being sold to pay a pressing grocery debt. Young, freshly trapped rabbits baked with seasoning, formed a large part of our diet – I would still rather have rabbit than chicken. At times, when vegetables were scarce, Mother boiled up ordinary vining nettles; they taste like spinach, and have a high food value. We had always been very poor so to us added hardship meant little or nothing; who would bother with butter when they could have Mother's bread spread with dripping and sprinkled with pepper and salt or perhaps spread thickly with moist sugar. Show me the bare-footed bush lad who isn't sorry for the poor boy who has to wear boots! We did not know we were poor. The most precious thing of all to a child is freedom, and in that we were millionaires; all that was best in Australia was ours, the bush land and our imagination made us kings of the world. It was many years later in life that I read Farewell to Fifth Avenue by Cornelius Vanderbilt Junior, and could not help contrasting his boyhood with my own. Son of one of the wealthiest and most envied families in the world he was, until manhood, as much a prisoner in that elaborate Fifth Avenue mansion as if he had been in Sing Sing.

Thirteen years old now, and some things called "Adenoids" or "Tonsils", or both, cropped up, and with them my first trip to Lithgow and hospital, and my first ride in a train. A few of the remaining impressions are the solemn ceremonial formula of buying the tickets – "Two Second Singles to Lithgow, please!" There was a feeling in the background of my consciousness that if the wrong words were uttered, social ostracism would result. Then a feeling of elation as we started, followed by some uneasiness as we gathered speed – (the wreck of the Melbourne Express at Benalong, with heavy loss of life was still a fresh memory – then the surgery of Dr. Gibbes; the hospital; pyjamas bought for the occasion (they were much too large); a philosophic acceptance of the anaesthetic; a journey among the constellations; a rude awakening; beastly throat, and lots of blood. Finally, the clean fresh look of Katoomba after soot-draped Lithgow. The throat healed and life settled down again.

A telephone message to say Norbert was coming home on final leave before sailing for France sent me running to tell Dad, who was splitting posts from a stringybark tree near Back Creek. Dad put down the mall and wedges without a word and came back with me. Norb looked taller than his six feet two in his manly uniform and Digger hat, and I had not truly known what pride was, until I saw him then. Just to be his young brother made me the biggest man in the world; not once did I doubt that he would come home with a V.C.

Next day took me out into the rain in search of waratahs for Norb to take away. Leave came to an end all too soon, and Mother's goodbye to her big son is still my greatest argument against war. Dad stood by, saying little, thinking much. There is a psychic streak in my Dad's family, and I have often wondered if the events of the following months were already casting their shadow, for within nine months Norb was resting from the brutality of war under a small cross near Menin Road, and Dad, too, was gone.

Back up in Narrowneck Range, behind Megalong, were old coal workings, tramways and machinery, deserted for some twenty years; trees were growing in between the sleepers of the tramway, and even between the corner posts and great block which marked the butcher's shop, erected when the mines were flourishing.

This was a favourite spot to me; lovely wildflowers

grew along the tramways, and waratahs and flannel flowers were banked about the sandstone benches lower down. The place was not easy to get to; miles of thick gum saplings, which had grown from the seedlings left after some ancient bush fire, made the way difficult to find and there was no track. Before leaving Megalong Valley, I ran out on a last quick visit. Things were moving quickly now; Mick followed Norb off to the war, and Ped followed quick. It was then decided to migrate the family to the Promised Land – Queensland. Dad rode off across country to Burragorang Valley, to say farewell to the remaining members of his family, and all his old friends. Packing commenced, and there was much discussion as to what should be left behind. All was set to go; Dad came home at midnight, and dawn saw him stricken with his last illness, but he lingered for some months.

We settled in Katoomba awhile, and then came my first contact with town schools – St. Canice's. Easter brought appendicitis, and appendicitis brought a second trip to Lithgow Hospital. I don't remember getting excited over my operation, but I do remember two days of burning thirst afterwards, and visions of the little cool waterfalls in Nellie's Glen.

At last, we were to go north. It was all arranged, and our passages were booked – second class, of course on the Brisbane Limited Express. I liked that word "Limited", though vague about its meaning. It seemed to add just one more touch of importance, if any were needed. The big day came, and we set out from Katoomba on the two o'clock train. "God speed you!" my old teacher had said, and we certainly were sped; rocking round those curves

A FAIRY'S PAINT BRUSH

I found a fairy's paint brush
And straight away I knew
That fairies had been painting flowers,
All the whole night through.

When other folks were sleeping
And Mr. Moon stood by,
The 'Little People' went to work,
Some in the Flame tree high.

They painted all the 'Wheels of Fire'
And Queensland Waratahs;
They painted little Flannel Flowers
And made them shine like stars.

They tinted all the creamy bells
That grow on 'Wonga vines';
They climbed and coloured orchids rare
That cling to lofty pines.

When birdies welcomed in the day
With many a silver song
The fairies crept into the flowers
And slept the whole day long.

The flowers are their houses
And they paint them every hue,
For fairies like their houses painted
Just the same as you.

on the Blue Mountains at more speed than I had ever known. Our heads never left the windows as new scenes flashed by. What a thrill was the first glimpse of Glenbrook Creek, and the old viaduct over Emu Plains. But bigger things were ahead – the Nepean River, the largest sheet of water I had yet seen, and beyond that regiment upon regiment of red-roofed houses, great buildings, lofty chimney stacks, and slender church steeples rising out of the golden smoke haze in the last sun of that winter's evening. There was magic in that first glimpse of Sydney; something which cannot be recaptured. Past suburban stations we flew with a rattle and flurry of lights, and then we emerged into a gleaming spiderweb of railway tracks, constellations of red and green lights, dozens of black hissing engines, and Central Station, its great roof arching over nineteen platforms. Brief were our glimpses of Sydney that night, for the Limited – with a capital "L" – was waiting for the twenty-eight hour run north, and soon we were climbing the hills towards Hornsby, with the great city glittering like the Milky Way behind us. Then at Rose's suggestion, we set out to explore the mysteries of our first corridor train. We pulled into Newcastle and a fresh engine was hooked at the back end of the train to pull us out of the dead end. For hours we had the impression that we were going back to Sydney. The Hawkesbury Bridge and the pies at Werris Creek were two other memories of that night.

Nine o'clock in the morning, and Wallangarra, and Queensland, and transhipping, and breakfast. Across the platform to pull our new train was a splendid engine of black, trimmed with burnished brass and with the Queensland Coat of Arms on his manly chest. On the side, also in glittering brass, was his name: "Sir William MacGregor". Such a handsome fellow certainly deserved a title! The immense cultivated acres of the Darling Downs, the countless windmills, the houses on stilts, and the hair-raising descent of the Toowoomba Range are the only vivid impressions which have remained of my first day in Queensland.

We went on to live in Sandgate, a seaside suburb of Brisbane, and here was my first glimpse of the sea. Going to the Christian Brothers' School in Brisbane and finding my first Queensland cobber, Pat, with snowy hair, are some of my first impressions of Queensland.

In the early spring of that year we buried our Dad. It is my great regret now, that Dad died when I was too young to appreciate him. He belonged to an era that has gone – my impression is that you cannot meet men like him any more, one of the full-bearded pioneers who helped to build Australia.

Dad's tales of the west – the west that is no more, when the bullock teams went to Bourke, when bushrangers and wild blacks and berri-berri fever added to the hazards of thirst, fire and flood – were tales gathered in nearly half a century spent beyond the fringe of civilization. These tales were often told around the glowing hearth when I was tiny; tales that would have filled a dozen volumes, but which now can never be recorded. Dad knew more than one bushranger by his first name. He was present at the shooting of the notorious bushrangers, Thurston and Angel. Through his stories ran a strong vein of native humour. I want to quote one little thing which happened three weeks before his last illness.

Dad was riding into Katoomba when a "go-getter" street photographer, thinking that he had a good prospect in a bearded bushman, jumped out with his camera saying, "Take your photo while you wait, Sir?"

Quick as a shot came Dad's reply, as he dug his heels into his old chestnut mare: "Take my photo while I'm going, young fellow."

Here is another true story, which will help further to show what manner of man he was.

Dad and Uncle Robert were taking a mob of cattle through heavily timbered country. Early one morning a steer disappeared. Dad rode back to look for it while Uncle took the mob on. About noon he caught up with my Uncle; he had a lovely wildflower in his hand, and his voice was enthusiastic, "Look, Robert," he said, "I've found a new flower – never seen anything like it in my life."

"Yes, it's a nice flower, Peter," answered the practical Robert, "but what about the steer?"

Peter had forgotten about the steer.

On a shelf above the fireplace were two greasy dog-eared books, the poets, Byron and Moore, which had gone on Dad's packsaddle who knows how many miles? Sometimes he took one or the other down and read his favourite verses in a deep, rumbling voice. One line comes back to my memory, as I picture that scene by the glow of the open fire "Silent O'Moyle, by the roar of thy waters " – something of Moore's.

I remember too, his quotation, the most apt quotation I have ever heard, when news came of the evacuation of Gallipoli. It was from Byron:

"The winds are high and Helles tide
Rolls darkly heaving to the main
And night's descending shadows hide
The field of blood bedewed in vain"

His rolling voice gave a deep solemn note to the family prayers by the fire at night; the lamp was always turned low, partly to prevent distraction by the everyday things about the room and partly to save expensive kerosene; leaping firelight in a darkened room can create a more impressive atmosphere than a high altar. Dad was broadminded in the best sense of the word; he never preached or ramped of what we should or should not do; like mother, it was by example that his lessons were taught. He had that deep, simple religion common to all men of the soil.

Many so-called thinkers seem to have a wrong impression of the settled religious thinking which usually goes hand in hand with the rural occupations. If a professor sees in his looking-glass a strong argument in favour of a Simian ancestry, the man on the land will possibly be interested in it, but only as a theory; all his life he has been battling with hard facts, not abstract thoughts and he knows what will happen to his land and how soon the bailiff will be in, if he starts running his farm along lines of unsubstantiated theory. His very life and work have given him a true perspective of the value of theories as such.

Generations of the land give men a settled outlook which is frequently mistaken for stodginess or stupidity by erratic thinkers, who follow the wavering trends of any new writer who happens to be fashionable for the moment. A farmer's life is conducive to clear, simple thinking which is unclouded by restless speculation. He sees in his everyday life the germination of seed, the opening of a rosebud, the birth of little calves and long-legged foals and he knows that all the greatest scientists of the generation and the hundreds of millions of pounds expended in research have not been able to reproduce, artificially, the simplest of these daily miracles. He knows that the humblest of his farm machines did not build itself nor can it run itself, so by cold irrefutable logic he does not expect that the mighty machinery of the universe and that vast complicated system which we call Nature, either built themselves or run themselves. There must have been a Builder and a General Manager whom he calls God.

Away up the Cox River, in the uninhabited country between Burragorang Valley and Jenolan Caves, is a splendid granite mountain, which, for upwards of seventy years, has been known as Peter O'Reilly's Range. Recently an enthusiastic group of people have tried to have it renamed "Mount Yellow Dog". Whatever may be the merits of the new name, there are many people who think with me that it should retain the name of a grand old pioneer – Peter O'Reilly, my father.

Dad had lived his whole life in the outdoors. The saddest days for him and for us, were those when he lay in his bed from which he would never rise. When we left him in that little hilltop cemetery, we were glad for his sake.

I often like to picture him up above where the good old pioneers go, with his bush mates who had gone before him, sitting round a comfortable camp fire which can never go out, with quartpots that are always full of tea, and old pipes that are always stoked with plug tobacco, yarning with their slow, rumbling voices about the days of the savage blacks and the wild cattle.

Two days after Dad's funeral, I tore up the front steps on my way home from school. I stopped at the door of our little sittingroom. Our old priest, Father Power, was standing with his hands behind his back. There was a piece of crumpled blue paper clenched in one hand; Mother was sitting forward in her chair, sobbing her heart out – big Norbert had been killed at Menin Road.

There was nothing to keep us in town now. Word came through that we were to leave Sandgate and go to join Tom and Herb on the plateau. I was the advance guard, and what a proud man I was, buying my ticket to Beaudesert. What a magic name "Beaudesert" was! It was the name on the envelopes of all the letters we had sent north since 1912.

A funny little mixed train – partly passenger, but mostly goods took me to Beaudesert. There were many shuntings and backings, and the journey of forty-seven miles took four and a half hours. The carriage ahead of ours carried first class passengers, the one behind us carried pigs for the Beaudesert saleyards, so by logic, I must have been travelling second class. A coach with four horses took me to Kerry, a fertile valley colonised by immigrants from Kerry, Ireland, over half a century before, and so green that it might have been a piece of the Emerald Isle that had mothered the pioneers.

That night was spent in rolling over in bed, thinking about the morrow, when I would ride up to that plateau of my dreams – dreams like those of the Norseman who dreamt of Valhalla. Tom was there to ride up with me next morning; Tom, another redheaded dreamer like myself, a man who loved his birds and flowers and trees as much as any man alive. If you look at the catalogue of Queensland trees you will find *Pittisporum oreillyii* – one of Tom's contributions to science.

Tom, like Herb, had wanted to go to the war, but the three young bloods had got in first, and someone had to stay to look after the family.

Midmorning saw us riding up through Kerry towards that great bulk of blue ranges, vast, silent, mysterious – the Promised Land, the wonderful plateau, that we had dreamed of day and night. Kerry was a joy to ride through that day.

Years later, on an Autumn day of blue and green, with an idle drift of white cloud, I was riding a wine-red bay horse and driving a mob of lazy, fat cattle through Kerry. It was a slow restful ride, and just the sort of day when one might lapse into poetry. The result was "Kerry, the Valley of Jewels" .

ॐ

Kerry – The Valley Of The Jewels

There was an old sailor named Sinbad,
Who told in his Arabic lore,
Of a beautiful valley of diamonds,
By a far-off ethereal shore.

I ne'er ever thought that his story
Was more than a fairy-tale grand,
Till I found my own valley of jewels
Right here in my own sunny land.

Where mountains of emerald rise upward
To a turquoise of blue up above,
With pearly white clouds drifting over
Kerry, the valley I love!

There are amethyst pools in the river
And cascades of opal-white foam,
While red coral tropical flowers
Bedower each settler's home.

The mornings in Kerry are sapphire,
And beryl the tone of the noon,
The evenings mellow to garnet,
Then, Mother o'pearl comes the moon.

When people of Kerry foregather
Each story they tell is a gem,
And though some of the folks are "rough diamonds",
They are REAL diamonds too, all of them.

The big thunderstorms of December,
Black opal, with red lightning fire,
Brings scenes of bejewelled splendour,
Beyond heart's greatest desire.

But best of all is the sunset,
All burning with ruby and gold,
`Twill burn a bright path in my memory,
Till I have grown feeble and old.

And then when the sunset has faded
There follows a night made of jet,
With stars blazing brighter than diamonds,
(Oh! God, let me never forget.)

❧

We rode up Stockyard Creek Gorge, which runs back into the range and here I saw my first tropical jungle. The impression was a deep vivid greenness; different from the grey-green of the Australian bush; like the vegetation of another planet. Down from the lush green of the trees hung ropes and festoons of leafy vines, away aloft were incredible tree gardens, tons of ferns and blooming orchids weighing down the huge boughs which supported the jungle roof. Great palm trees reared their umbrella tops aloft. The jungle floor was a delicate, intricate embroidery of contrasting greens which were countless varieties of fern; all the conservatories of the world rolled into one.

Here and there, as if to remind us that we were still in Australia, grew a peerless flooded gum, taller and whiter than a Grecian column, making a dramatic foil for the unearthly green of the jungle.

Tom pointed out the parasitical fig trees which start at the top of a tree from seed dropped by birds, and throw down a lattice work of cordlike roots. These roots increase in size and finally strangle and kill the parent tree. The fig, then assuming command, grows rapidly, and when the victim rots away, towers upwards with an open lattice trunk, like the mast of a U.S.A. battleship. This is only one of the unearthly forms of life which go to make up the jungle.

Soon we heard a harsh rasping call, and looking up I had my first glimpse of a bird of paradise, the rifle bird, velvety black, with shot colours of blue and green as brilliant as stainless steel. The beating of his wings in flight was like the rustling of a heavy satin dress. The female of the species is plain, as is the case with most brilliant birds – a provision of wise Nature, which prevents the attraction of enemies during the nesting season.

Now we left the bed of the gorge and climbed out of the jungle and up the range, on a track which led through ironbark and casuarina trees. Redbacked wrens fluttered like living rubies from the high kangaroo grass. By the track grew grass trees twenty feet high, with their white flower spikes pointing towards heaven like giant candles; blood red honeyeaters worked on them, sipping honey through awl-like bills. Higher we climbed while the wooded gorge fell away to the left, and the dark green pine trees on the opposite range made a serrated skyline.

Here, slung between trees fifteen feet apart, was a web of the great yellow spider; a tough network, sticky as rubber solution, it sometimes traps small birds. Should you be so unwise as to ride through it your hat may be pulled off and your eyelids gummed down, causing much discomfort until the web is washed off.

Across the gorge, lyrebirds, a mile apart, answered one another with their ringing throaty calls. Two great seven foot eagles swept in close as they spiralled upwards. Australians, be proud of your wedgetail eagle, for he is the largest and fiercest eagle in the world; the true monarch of the air.

Higher climbed the track; the same which the big boys had cut out in 1915. Now, it was going boldly round the face of a great volcanic cliff, where a stone rolled over the edge would go for a thousand feet. Higher still, until we were looking down on the pair of eagles. Then we twisted in our saddles and looked back over the forty miles of swelling pastoral country, to the blue ranges beyond. In a clearing at the top of the range stood the slab hut where lived Cousins Pat and Luke. From the inkweed and thistles along the timber edge rose a cloud of parrots, deep crimson and rich blue. It is not without reason that our crimson rosella has been called the most beautiful of all birds.

He is friendly, too, and will come into your garden if encouraged by an occasional handful of wheat. Another way is to allow a few thistles to grow near the house. Some day I would like to go to the Amazon country and on to the Orinoco Delta and see how a flock of flamingoes would compare with a cloud of our parrots or our western galahs.

There was some more timber between Luke's clearing and ours, so that when we reached the rangetop where our house now stands, it was sunset – my first Queensland mountain sunset. There had been light cirrus clouds in regular rows, and the blazing afterglow transformed it into a ploughed field of fire. Etched inky black against it was the western skyline, a mass of great sawtooth ranges, and stretching from our feet out to the ranges were rolling foothills, ridge beyond ridge like the giant billows of some misty, purple sea. For more than twenty years I have lived with that western view, and it is still fresh and wonderful to me each morning; partly, perhaps, because it is never the same. I am looking across over it now from my lounge windows as I write, and its cloud masses and light and shadow effects have completely changed in the last twenty minutes. The ever changing foreground, too – the great iridescent green butterflies that drift by the windows, the honeyeaters that flutter to the clematis on the porch, the scarlet and green king parrots in the shrubbery outside – all help to add a transient effect to that vast background. And which way in the great procession of moods and colours do I like it best? There can be no single favourite, since the essence of its appeal to me is its limitless variety, but perhaps amongst the most beautiful would be when the early morning is upon it. The great valleys filled with lakes of snowy mist with the ice-blue peaks rising beyond; their crests touched with the first rosy light of day; or maybe on a winter's evening, purple mountains against a dazzling, saffron sky, a yellow green light over all; or again half smothered in torn, racing white clouds, cyclone-driven, now screening, now revealing; or perhaps just as I first saw it.

Tom and I sat in our saddles until the colour had faded, and then we rode quickly down to the little slab hut on Moran's Creek. The kookaburras were having their goodnight laugh as we unsaddled. Herb had the Billy boiling and potatoes cooked. Their old black cat, Beelzebub, put up his back and spat at me. We got to be good friends later, and he lived to the ripe old age of twenty-five years. That night I was assigned to Norb's bunk – my new life had begun.

I had hoped then that some day I would be big enough, physically and otherwise, to fill Norb's place. Neither hope has been realised. A hundred yards from the hut was a little waterfall with a merry voice. It sang me to sleep that night and every night during the years we lived in that old hut, and when the time came to move to our new house on top of the range, I missed my waterfall more than words can tell. I wonder if the song composers who write so glibly of cottages by waterfalls truly understand the companionship by day and peace by night, which the voice of a waterfall can bring – not the roar and boom of a great torrent, but the soothing restfulness of a gay little fellow in a small creek?

Behind the hut was a little track through the big timber to the creek. It was our water track. Over it spread a huge tamarind, and a eugenia tree, and in the berry season, wongas and little green pigeons – quieter than domestic fowls – fed on the fallen berries, and did not trouble to get out of the way as we carried our buckets of water up to the hut.

CHAPTER VIII

Re-establishment –
With the Home Fire Kept Burning

N O boy in the world, it seemed, was ever more fortunate than I, in the new rough life of that little clearing, in the heart of one hundred square miles of great unexplored ranges, and gorges of lofty timber, of fern and palm, orchid and vine, peopled by the most glorious birds in the world.

Now may I tell you something of those birds which have been my neighbours all these years? Mention of Australian birds should begin with the kookaburra. Jack is like the "digger" – the gamest of his tribe. No one who has ever seen Jack tackle and kill a big tiger snake would hesitate to recommend him for the V.C., and whenever you see sturdy bush kiddies running barefoot to school, remember that their safety is largely due to Jack, the Snake Killer. But most of all, we love Jack for his sense of humour. One morning years ago in our old bush school beyond the Blue Mountains – it was Monday morning, and the teacher's wrath hung over us like a thundercloud – the teacher was hurrying across the room, probably to chastise some fractious pupil, and she kicked her toe and hurt it. Not one kiddy was game to even grin, but from a gum tree outside a kookaburra shook the hills with laughter; these are the kind of situations which appear to delight him. Perhaps you are out riding, your horse falls and you get a buster. As you pick yourself up out of the dust and finger a skinned nose, a loud laugh breaks out overhead. Or perhaps your car gets bogged in the black soil. As you lie down in the sticky mess, trying to put chains on the tyres, Kooka up in an ironbark laughs so heartily that he attracts half a dozen others to his tree, and they laugh in chorus till the ridges echo. The stricken motorist usually finishes by joining in – if he has any sense of humour left.

Now let me tell you of the lyrebird, one of Australia's greatest mimics, and one of the world's most remarkable birds.

The Albert Lyrebird of the jungles of Queensland has not quite such a magnificent tail as his southern cousin, *Novae hollandae,* but his call is, I think, richer and clearer, and he is a better mimic than the southern bird. His repertoire includes not only every major bird call, but the sounds of wood chopping, howling of dingoes, barking of dogs, crying of babies, the drag of a crosscut saw and the clinking of wedges. Twenty-five yards from my little cottage a lyrebird has a dancing ground, and he calls there on every winter's morning. These birds are very plentiful in this region, which is remarkable when you consider that they live and breed almost entirely on the ground, that dingoes and tiger cats are also plentiful, and that the female lyrebird lays but one egg a year.

Writing of mimics brings to mind the Satin bowerbirds which have their playgrounds all around where I live. They give some very good imitations, including a very human "coo-ee"' which may have been handed down through bird generations since the days when the black warriors sent their signal calls echoing through the jungle and down the ravines. The Satin bird, which gets its name from the handsome purple satin coat which the male bird dons when seven years old, is mainly famous for his bower, or playground.

It consists of two graceful walls built of sticks, and is elaborately decorated with wild flowers, snake skin, small shells and any other bush curios he can find. These birds are partial to the colour blue, so you will usually find blue flowers and berries in their playgrounds, and woe betide your garden if you grow blue Delphinium or Larkspur. Blue disinfectant bottles are also in demand, and two blue bags taken from our washhouse were found in a bower over a mile away.

Another lovely bowerbird which lives near my home – he frequently comes into the vine which trails over our porch – is the Golden Regent bird.

He is coloured with equal parts of gold and velvety black, and to see him fly up in the sunlight before you is a sight you could never forget. He is lazy and his bower does not compare with that of the Satin as an architectural effort, but he is an ardent collector of all yellow or golden feathers and curios and it is easy to tempt him into your garden if you grow yellow flowers. Close beside our present home, Goblin Wood, is a splendid Purple Satin's playground; it is a bare twenty yards from our garden, his principal source of supply. This bird is not merely an opportunist, he is socialist; he allows a Golden Regent the freedom of his bower, the Regent plays in it and brings his yellow flowers and feathers but no one seems to mind the clash in colour schemes.

In North Queensland they have the unique toothbill and the glorious golden bowerbird; the latter is a true artist. His bower is a large elaborate affair beautifully decorated with mosses. These birds I have not seen but I am very familiar with the spotted bowerbird west of the Divide, the best collector of them all. Spotty has no colour complex; all things quaint or bright go his way and his collection may range from household crockery to a bleached skull. An old prospector told me that in alluvial country it is always worthwhile to visit Spotty's playgrounds, many valuable slugs of gold have been found in the bowers. To Spotty, too, must go the distinction of being Australia's best mimic; he is more versatile than the lyrebird.

It is a common practice among bowerbirds, more especially the Satin, to paint the walls of their bower. This is usually accomplished by masticating charcoal which, mixed with saliva, is run through the side of the bird's beak on to the sticks which form the walls of the bower. Near civilisation however, the Satin bowerbird usually does his painting with stolen blue bags.

ès

Mother, who had been a fearless horsewoman most of her life, had lost her riding balance through a dreadful operation two years earlier. This meant that, when she came to join us on the plateau, she had to walk the seven miles from the old Stockyard Creek waggon road, up the big climb to home. We thought her wonderful then, considering the long strain and sadness of Dad's illness, the shock of losing her beloved son, and also her own trouble. Dozens of times in the years that followed she repeated the walk; the last time, twenty years after that first effort, the shade temperature was over a hundred degrees, and Mother was then seventy-five years of age.

Life in that old humpy was something that would be hard to parallel now. There were two rooms, one for sleeping and keeping clothes, the other was a cooking, eating and living room, which also had a couple of bunks. These bunks were made by putting two poles lengthways through chaff bags, and were supported at each end by two short crossed legs wired X fashion; mattresses were two chaff bags sewn together and stuffed with soft, pungent kangaroo grass. There was a large open fireplace, paved with uneven stones; there is no smooth flat stone on Green Mountains. Care had to be taken in the selection of stones for the fireplace as some of our volcanic rock is highly explosive when exposed to fire.

At night the fire was banked; a nugget of burning Mariara wood was buried in hot coals and then completely covered with ashes. In the morning when the ashes were raked away the nugget would be the same size and shape, but transformed into a mass of live, glowing coal. From the time when the family arrived at the humpy in 1917 until we left it in 1925, the fire on the hearth was not once out.

Cooking was done over the open fire; frying pans had long wooden extensions to their handles to allow standing back; billycans for boiling stews, vegetables and tea water were hung on chains and wire hooks over the blaze. Jam roly-polys, puddings and joints of corned beef were boiled in kerosene tins, while dampers, scones, cakes and roasts of meat were cooked in the camp oven. There are few camp ovens left outside of droving outfits and their use is almost a lost art. A camp oven looks like a shallow, flatbottomed, three-legged pot of cast iron with a large lid like a coolie hat, upturned at the edges to hold the red coals which are piled on top of it; the oven is hung over a slow fire, but there must be no great difference between the heat above and below, otherwise your cooking will end disastrously. Mother's camp oven cooking was something I shall always like to think about. All other members of the family, more especially the boys, were experts in its use. Damper, which with corned beef and Billy tea, has played a major part in the pioneering of Australia, is in fact a circular flat loaf of bread concocted of ordinary scone mixture and baked quickly.

The original Australian damper was baked in hot ashes without the aid of a camp oven. This was indeed a rare craft, learned in the hard school of trial and error; Tom could cook them that way and Dad had been an expert. It is unfortunate that the origin of the name "damper" has been lost in the rapid moving of our brief history.

The tamarind trees which grew behind the humpy had pretty brown berries in midsummer. We crushed the berries and added water and sugar. The result was a very pleasant summer drink, at least, so we thought in those days, before Tom's Lisbon lemons began to bear.

The dairy cattle had been brought up the cliff track from Stockyard Creek. The final stage of the journey, instead of taking a day as expected, took two. The cows were quiet but never having seen big timber before, were hot and sulky when the lower timber was reached and scattered in all directions into it. We tied up our horses as it was impossible to ride them through the vines, and went in after the cattle on foot, bringing out a few at a time to the track, but by the time we had brought out a second lot, the first would have gone in again. This went on for hours, the cattle becoming more and more bad tempered owing to Gympie stings and the rips of thorny vines. It was late when we got them through to the open grass at the range foot, and when darkness came we bedded them down on a grassy ledge half way up the climb.

We spent the night with the cattle; it was a weird night; there were cliffs above and below our ledge, and we, knee-deep in soft kangaroo grass, seemed to be caught in some ethereal grazing land between earth and sky. Overhead were a myriad stars, dim with the haze of that soft summer night. The cattle champed contentedly, and whiptail wallabies thumped about, resentful of these new intruders on their pasture.

Around us in the eucalyptus and casuarina trees were those night sounds familiar to the people of the outdoors; the chuckling of blue possums, the cry of koalas and flying phalangers (those creatures which are erroneously called squirrels, are really flying possums).

Away across the gorge from the jungle which clothed Cainbable Range came the friendly call of a mopoke and now and then the howl of a dingo, a sound which might easily have emanated from a damned soul. There was another cry, too, late at night, from the jungle a mile away, a thin high wail, which none of us could identify, but which we have facetiously named the Stockyard Creek Banshee. Almost every time I have ridden the Stockyard Creek track at night the "Banshee" has wailed from the far side of the gorge; it has never been heard by us anywhere else. Some suggest that it might be the earthbound spirit of a black warrior – be that as it may, it is not the only uncanny thing about the gorge.

Daylight came with the rollicking laughter of the kookaburra, and the ringing dawn call of the Yellow Robin. We counted the cattle to see if any were missing; instead we had one extra. Toady had a small, red, bull calf which we named Roger, and ever after the little neck of the ridge where he was born was known as Roger's Saddle. We continued the drive, Tom carrying Roger across the front of his saddle, and Toady following behind with anxious little moans. (Roger, by the way, had been named because his natal bed had been a trampled mass of Stinking Roger).

Nearing the cliff, Herb took a few head of cattle on as leaders, and the rest followed across Moran's Creek amongst the logs, inkweed,. It was an anxious time; if the cattle became terrified and piled up on the narrow cliff track, many of them would have been forced over the edge to their destruction far below. It is a difficult matter to induce a large mob of cattle to walk single file around a strange cliff track, but it was done without loss, though luck must have been with us that day; since then many head have been killed over the cliffs.

We kept Toady near the humpy and Roger in a little dingo-proof enclosure of saplings. Toady supplied the first luxury on Green Mountains – milk for our tea, the first in seven years. The rest of the herd had been turned out in the clearing and paspalum, higher than their backs. Strange to look across a small clearing, knowing that there were many cattle in it, and yet not see one.

The horses were in the high grass too; fat, round-backed fellows with barely enough work to keep them docile. A flash horse regards work in the same light as a truant does school. It is strange in these days of subdividing fences to think of the hours and the curses spent in running in horses. It is small wonder that we often thought of walking to Kerry as a less arduous alternative. Some subtle telegraph seemed to warn the horses when they were to be run in; they hid in the high grass with not a stamp or champ to give away their position, and were only located after the desperate searcher had climbed many high springboard stumps which served as reconnaissance towers. When approached they went into action with arched necks and streaming tails, their glossy backs flashing like mirrors as they stampeded through a labyrinth of logs to the far corner of the clearing, there to take up another stand in Stinking Roger twelve feet high. In these stampedes they were led by Baldy and Nutty who, as colts, ran on vast unfenced acres of the Darling Downs. Nutty, in particular, had been enjoying a long period of freedom while his master, Mick, was in France. The horses were mostly good ones and when the bridle was finally put on them could carry one for the fifty-two mile return trip to Beaudesert without showing noticeable fatigue.

All of this time Tom and Herb had been going forward with the building of the cow yard, bails and calf pen. Of the vast variety of jungle trees, only two, Crows Ash and Lignum Vitae were suitable for fencing, all others used to rot in the ground; fortunately both were good splitters and soon there were enough posts, rails and slabs for the job. The price of galvanized roofing iron for the buildings had then reached its prohibitive wartime peak; but even had we been able to buy it, we had not then the time or manpower for packing it from Kerry, so the roofs of the milking shed and the separating room were thatched. Packhorse loads of coarse blady grass were brought over from the cliff edge and tied into position with homemade stringybark rope. Farm machinery was very scarce at that time, and we had to pay a high price for a secondhand cream separator; Herb packed it up the range on Blogs. Cream cans were almost as dear as if they had been made of silver, but butter prices, too, were proportionately high, so it was not an inopportune time to start dairying.

Even before things were in readiness, the calves began to arrive; little wobbly-kneed red and roan fellows which mostly had to be carried home. Roger's little pen became congested and all the young generation were transferred to the new enclosure. One of our great difficulties was the finding of newly born calves in high paspalum. After calving, a cow will hide its calf, returning only occasionally to give it a drink. When approached she will invariably walk off, bellowing, in the opposite direction to that of the calf; the searcher, if he is new at the game, will be deceived by this piece of strategy, and led on a fine, wild goose chase. Logs and weeds added to the difficulty, and many hours were lost looking for calves in those first days.

We had a blue cattledog which we called Superfluous Hound for obvious reasons; he was a hindrance rather than a help and we kept him only for the sake of having a dog round the house.

Gradually the dairy took shape; the calves were weaned and taught to drink separated milk out of a bucket. The cows settled down to their routine of being milked twice a day. The novelty of the cream separator wore off; when it was new we all fought for the honour of turning it, but after a month nobody wanted to. Those incurable mimics, the lyrebirds, added a new sound to their repertoire, the bawling of poddy calves.

There were loud cheers when our first consignment of cream was sent away to the butter factory. A six gallon can was fastened to the hooks of the packsaddle on either side of Blogs. The lid of each can had to be bound with cloth so that the cream would not leak out during the journey. We watched the caravan out of sight; Herb was riding Baldy and leading Blogs on a long halter, the cans rocked gently like the "roll" of an ocean liner; Baldy, cheated out of his usual privilege of bucking when first mounted (Herb had a strong hold of him) minced along, relieving his spleen by switching his tail like a propeller.

Before the gorge was reached, there was a telltale "slosh" of butter milk from the cans, which told that Blogs with his rolling gait had churned the cream to butter. Since this was to have been the ultimate fate of the cream anyhow, we thought that the butter factory people would have been pleased to be saved the trouble, but not they, we were actually awarded only second class for our cream – a great disgrace, and all because it was churned!

Our cream stand was on Kerry road eight miles from home, and there the cream was picked up by horse coach. That historic trip was the forerunner of twenty odd years of packing cream; it still goes on today. Those were lonely, quiet trips; four hours the eight miles took, for the cream had to be taken quietly, otherwise it would have churned, and we found that sending butter to a butter factory was very bad form indeed.

The trips were nearly always at night with two packhorses; the reins and leading ropes clutched in one hand and a hurricane lantern in the other.

Going round the cliff track there always seemed to be just a tiny, self contained world within the lantern light, and the rest an immeasurable void of blackness. Bats would descend from their shelters, volcanic blowholes in the dark cliff, and circle the light, frightening the horses; great white moths would come from the darkness – flutter briefly and pass on to their limbo. Night creatures screeched or howled, or called softly according to their nature. It is strange that in the jungle, creatures which call by day are almost without exception musical or soothing; while the cries of the nocturnals, with the exception of two or three, could be collectively described as horrible. The great rain forest glooms majestically, crushingly, at night, and the lone horseman with his dim lantern, seems such a tiny, insignificant part of things. After twenty-five years of solitary night packing, it is just as strong – that feeling of being crushed and subdued by the vastness of the black world about me.

But the jungle had other moods; spring nights when the light of a great white moon cut sharply down through the trees and the warm air was heavy with the perfume of orchid and jasmine; those were nights when we lingered outside the humpy after the horses were let go, loth to break the spell. There were nights too, of storm and wind, when the great trees bent over like an archer's bow, and the wild scene was lit by flares of lightning. There was loneliness on those rides and sometimes fear, but never monotony. Not only did we boys take our turn on the pack trail, but Rose, who could handle her string of packhorses as capably as any man I have ever seen, brought home her team on black nights more often than I would care to remember.

Herb went to Brisbane that year to see the Minister for Works of the day, and renew the question of a road to our mountain. The word he brought back, though not very convincing, was nevertheless heartening, for when there is no other chance we are prone to hang our hopes on very slender threads.

I began to visualise a swift end to the packing era, and picture a smooth, scenic highway winding up the gorges and climbing along the wooded ranges to terminate at our door. Well it was for my big hopes, that I could not glimpse along the next quarter of a century and see the packing that lay before us.

December brought a thrilling and terrifying experience – my first tropical storm. It came just after darkness, with a continuous blaze of violet coloured lightning, which writhed incessantly across the sky, weaving never-ending patterns, branching out like the trees of a dead forest. With it, too, came green clouds rolling and twisting, driven by a hurricane which roared like something attending the ruin of the world. The old humpy shivered as from earthquake shock, but within twenty minutes all was calm again. It went as quickly as it had come.

One Sunday we went for a walk out to Norb's humpy; it was a sad little excursion. The dust of the pin borers was deep on the floor and table; under the bunk were his axe and brush hook, where he had laid them aside when his country called. Out in the circular clearing with its beetling walls of rain forest was an orchard which he had planted with high hopes, and some of the trees were already bearing fruit. He had brought those trees twenty miles by packhorse, even as he had done the roofing iron for the humpy. By the door an old-fashioned rose bush was blooming; it is still blooming though more than twenty-five years have gone since it was planted by him.

It must have been about Christmas time that we went there, for I remember the scarlet embothriums (Queensland Waratahs) were blooming at the clearing edge. Like every other small clearing, Norb's was a paradise for birds; noble scarlet and green King Parrots rose in a cloud as we entered; birds find these "man-made windows" to be rich feeding grounds as well as good sunbathing places.

There were pigeons too, topknots, baldies, browns and wongas, and an occasional wampoo – that miracle of purple and green, to which the naturalist, in an expansive mood, has given the vernacular name of magnificent fruit pigeon. I remember too, a breathtaking flash of gold which was my first view of a Regent bowerbird. They proved later to be very partial to clearings and second growth.

There is an undefinable something about Christmas which gives a tone of excitement and gaiety to the humblest of scenes. Even a crude slab home on a mountain selection became an enchanted grotto of green for our first Queensland family Christmas. The walls were screens of glossy bosistoa; smoke blackened beams were twined and hidden by wild wisteria. There were highlights of rose mahogany berries and coral sprays of the flame tree. How gay we were and what a scene to look back upon in after years. Christmas observation has lost a great deal through modern sophistication; people who have not known the simple joys of a traditional Christmas have missed one of the bigger things of life.

No one could ever make a Christmas pudding as well as Mother (of course no man worth his salt could think otherwise of his Mother's pudding). There were nuts and sweets too, and passionfruit from the wild vine by the little creek; there were three kinds of wild raspberries, and jellies cooled by setting their basins in the cold running water of the creek; added to these were pints of thick, rich cream – the butter factory people must have wondered why we shipped short next day.

We had ordered a leg of lamb, but when it arrived green and smelly after the two days' journey from Beaudesert, it was given to Superfluous Hound, who decided quite correctly that Christmas had indeed come. That is why our dinner passed without a variation from the eternal corned meat. There were of course wild turkeys and pigeons which fed almost up to the door, but there was a sacred trust laid upon us to protect them and we each had little cardboard certificates to prove that we were honorary rangers. Besides you don't go killing and eating your friends and only neighbours just because you feel like a change of diet.

No place, whether it be humpy or palace could be home to Mother without a few fowls and ducks. We brought up two packhorse loads, packed two to a cornbag with holes cut for their heads to poke out; they looked very odd and the horses snorted threateningly, but all arrived safely. Since that day thousands have arrived by the same method.

It was a little before Christmas that we made our first trip to the summit of the green Border Range and visited the lookout points of Mt. Bethongabel (pronounced Bethongabell), and Mt. Wanungra; these were airy, orchid fringed balconies on the rim of two thousand foot cliffs which dropped into the valley of the Tweed River. The whole north eastern corner of New South Wales was spread out like a huge relief map, nearly four thousand feet below; dark green paspalum threaded with blue rivers, with here a town and there great rectangles of pale green which were sugarcane fields. To the east was the vast blue ocean and away to the south the cream semicircle of Byron Bay, where restless lines of white showed that the tireless Pacific rollers curled up and smashed themselves into snowy spray against the great arc of beach.

These lookout points and their tracks had been opened up by Herb, Norb and Mick in 1912. The track which they cut from Bethongabel to Wanungra traversed the most beautiful forest I have ever seen; it is entirely draped with long green moss and lichen, its treeferns are loftier and nobler than any others on the range and its only large trees are the patriarchs of our forest, the ancient Antarctic Beeches *(Nothofagus moorei)*. These are reputed to be thirty centuries old, and when you see them you find that estimate easy to believe. There is something venerable about them that makes you want to take off your hat and stand in silence. Centuries of erosion have bared their great, gnarled root systems and with decay have opened up mysterious grottoes, making it possible for people to walk under the tree proper, through hanging masses of delicate film fern and dewy glow-worm threads. The tree itself, deeply pitted with decay and studded with giant bracket-fungus, is hung with long moss and grey "beard" lichen as a last touch to make the patriarchal figure complete. There is something about the atmosphere of a great antarctic Beech; something which must be experienced to be appreciated. Even more than the sense of its eerie appearance is the feeling that you are standing beside a live thing which was alive ten centuries before the birth of Christ.

For more than half the year, the mountain is hooded with cloud, and wraiths of white vapour pass through the moss-hung trees. From the dim tree caverns with their root stalactites come the call of the atrichornis – the mystery bird which can be heard but not seen, and from the moss above, the elusive ventriloquial cry of the olive whistler. If ever there was a goblin forest, surely it is the Antarctic Beech Forest of Bethongabel.

The Beech owes its name to the discovery of some of its timber preserved in glacier ice on the Antarctic continent. There were obviously forests of it there prior to the last ice age, though of course no plant life save lichen survives on that continent today. There are a few small stands of Nothofagus in the world today, and their distribution is as mysterious as their appearance – all are in forbidding mountain regions; the west coast of Tasmania, South Island of New Zealand, the rain forests of Patagonia and the loftiest ridge of the McPherson Range.

There is something more which I believe is not on scientific record. The beech forest, like the foundation of its contemporary, Solomon's Temple, is crumbling; every year sees another patriarch go back to earth, but there are no young trees coming on to take their places. The senile forest is with us today, but it belongs to yesterday, and when the "old men" fall, they are replaced by sassafras, wymania and embothrium. True, I have seen healthy young trees, but all were far removed from their parent forests. After almost every rainy season countless beech seedlings spring up, but of all these myriads not one survives the following summer. Perhaps the centuries have brought climatic changes unfavourable to the young trees, but my theory is that the parent trees are too ancient for successful reproduction. To me they are like the Parthenon or the ruined temples of Syria, splendid relics of a glory that has been, but they belong to the past, and cannot be revived any more than the civilisations of Mesopotamia or Egypt.

There is a lovely orchid in the beech country, to which some of the mystery of the forest attaches. It is very plentiful, in the border ranges, but grows only on beech trees. I have not yet seen the orchid on any tree, other than a beech, nor have I seen a beech tree without the orchid. Science proved it to be a new orchid. Though our boys had known it since 1911, it was described only in 1918 by Mr. Cyril White, Government Botanist, who was camped at Mt. Bethongabel that year with a large party of naturalists. It was a Dendrobium, and Mr. White gave it the specific name of "Fagi-Cola" in deference to the beech tree.

January, 1918, brought our first cyclone. This time the old humpy had to withstand a barrage lasting twenty-four hours. Herb nailed and barricaded the door, and we entered and left the humpy through a shutter window at the back. The cyclone unroofed our little dairy, and choked miles of our only track to civilisation with smashed timber. We thought then we were badly off. It was not until days later that we heard that up along the Queensland coast the same cyclone had wrecked the city of Mackay, killing many people.

Following the cyclone we had twenty-eight consecutive days of rain. Usually the dawn brought a cloudless sky, then, after sunrise, great golden clouds would billow up from behind the green border ranges; with the roar of rain on the jungle leaves, and a flashing double rainbow in their van, they would come charging down upon us as we sat milking in the mud under the stark timbers of our unroofed buildings; flocks of currawongs and parrots would rise crying from the inkweed. The moisture and mould seeped through the cracks into the humpy, and, it seemed, into our very souls.

The miles of pack track became miles of soft mud, knee-deep in places; the cliff section was dangerous and frequently blocked by rock falls; the cream trips were long stretches of sodden, interminable mud. Had we known it, that month was but a baptism; something to test us and fit us out for the packing and work in more than twenty rainy seasons to come. Once you have faced an ordeal and come through it well, its like can never trouble you again. That, perhaps is why the memory of that first rainy season is clearer than those of more than a score that followed; events that were hardships in that first year became ordinary, commonplace affairs ever after. Not one of us, Rose included, would now think it unusual or difficult to ride all night in the rain with packhorses or to take a string of horses down the cliff track in the face of a violent tropical thunderstorm, or to ride miles through big timber in a screaming cyclone; we have worked day and night in the worst that weather can do, and, thanks to that early baptism, the elements have nothing more with which to trouble us.

1918 too, saw Mick home from the war, still an invalid, but cheerful and full of yarns. He had come home via America and the Panama Canal and his kit bag was full of foreign coins and souvenirs. For days we did not work between milkings, just sat around and talked to Mick. After six months of convalescence Mick was discharged from military hospital and at the same time honourably discharged from the A.I.F.

He applied for and was ultimately given the post of working overseer of Lamington National Park. For the first time, the protection of the park wild life devolved upon an official instead of being the personal responsibility of the O'Reilly family. This appointment, however, lasted only about two years.

In November 1918 I was the herald of glorious news. I had made a record trip back from Kerry with the packhorses to tell the family that the war was over. We all know now what that news meant in most of the great cities of the world, but to us in the little slab hut that night it meant simply that Ped, a machine gunner in action, had ceased fire and would come back to us unhurt.

It was also in 1918 that I first found a scrub turkey's nest; the nest consists of a huge mound, a natural incubator, five feet high, built of mulch and rotting leaves, the heat of which incubates the eggs, which are buried in the mound. The egg is extraordinarily large, and development inside of it goes on to such an extent that after incubation the chick can scratch its way out of the mound and fend for itself in life.

Spring of that year brought countless cream, shell-pink and mauve orchids all along the western cliffs. Scrub wrens hung their green moss nests on low branches over the creeks. Yellow robins built artistic little homes decorated with coloured lichen – built them in bushes of bristlelike thorn so that the lizards could not climb up and eat the eggs; lovely sky blue eggs which matched the artistry of the nest.

The end of 1918 saw our horses very busy transhipping a large party of naturalists up to our range.

There was nothing new about this; for some years my brothers had conducted many scientists and nature lovers to their mountain paradise. These people were lodged in the various slab humpies of the selections, and formed the nucleus of the large tourist flow which our mountain now attracts. These scientists added a store of technical knowledge to the fund of practical nature lore which we had acquired.

In 1919 it was my good fortune to be chosen as

guide and camp-follower to Mr. Sid W. Jackson, a prominent ornithologist from Sydney, in his expedition to our ranges for the purpose of clearing up the secret of the "mystery bird", atrichornis. I learned much about the mystery bird, a dark brown, mouselike creature, which lives its secluded life under piles of fallen timber and lines its nest with a wood-pulp cardboard of its own manufacture.

Those months of close association with this versatile, practical naturalist accomplished a great deal in furthering my knowledge, not only of ornithology, but of kindred studies. As well as our atrichornis, which proved to be new, Mr. Jackson's visit added to science a new subspecies of olive-whistler, a mellow voiced creature which lives amongst the moss and treeferns on the loftiest part of our mountain.

I would like to mention here that the two earliest scientific visitors to our mountain were Mr. Henry Tryon, veteran Queensland entomologist, and the late Doctor John Shirley, who had many scientific interests, but specialised in botany. Another visitor whose periodical trips brought us great pleasure was Hilda Giessmann, of Mount Tamborine, who came with her big camera when the birds were nesting and the orchids blooming. Her bird and orchid studies are well known beyond Australia.

Ped came home in 1919, fit and brown; there was a merry reunion, no one seemed to remember the two vacant chairs, but just the same there was nobody who forgot. With our two soldiers home, hope began to run high for the long-wished-for road. Roads were being built to adjacent mountains with lesser scenic attractions. A Main Roads Board was created and our plateau was one of the first points visited by the new chairman; he pronounced the scenery to be the finest he had yet seen. This was indeed good food for optimism.

However, when it became obvious that nothing would be done, Ped left and took a post in New Guinea where he lived for many years. From then on we saw him only or brief periods of leave every two years. He has now joined the new A.I.F.

The years brought many lone exploring trips for me; it could not have been otherwise with a vast mysterious unexplored empire which began at the very edge of our clearings. The most successful of the early explorations was the discovery and traverse of Tooloona Creek. A perfectly graded track, one of a vast network constructed by the Queensland Forest Service now takes you through the heart of Tooloona Gorge and seasoned world tourists have pronounced it to be the most beautiful creek they have ever seen. But my proudest exploring moment came later; one winter afternoon, when l stood in a narrow stream bed between towering basalt cliffs the first white man to enter Black Canyon. In front of me the river leapt from a concealed chasm high up in the cliff, from the left, Lightning Falls poured in a snowy zigzag down the black rock, five hundred feet of misty, lacelike beauty, to tumble into the same turbulent pool which received the leaping, white water of the river.

It was late in 1920 that Mother bought a stove for us in Brisbane, and in due course it was delivered at the end of the waggon road. Our feelings about it were a little mixed; there was that pride of new ownership and with it serious anxieties and doubts as to whether we would ever get it safely to the top of the plateau.

Many years before, a neighbour of Dad's had taken a piano four miles down a bridle path to his home on Cox's River, below Megalong Valley. He had used two strong poles with their front ends through shaft harness on a cart horse, the piano was slung between the poles behind the horse, and the rear ends of the poles were manned by a few strong neighbours. It was an ingenious idea but it took a lot of sweat and language to carry it out.

We had thought to do something similar with our stove; we weren't quite sure how we would manage it; there had been no precedent for many of our transport problems and we had long been accustomed to devising means of carrying out a job as we went along. So we set out for Stockyard Creek, Tom, Mick and I; we had an axe for cutting poles and also that favourite standby, some fencing wire. There is a bush saying, that there is nothing a selector cannot accomplish given abundant wire and greenhide. A spare packhorse was brought too, just in case, and some spanners to pull the stove to pieces if necessary. Arrived at the job we cut the poles and spent some time experimenting to get the distribution of the weight correct. There was, as always, some argument. Each man had hit upon a separate idea and each was sure that his own was the only possible way of doing it.

Finally it was found that with one man leading the horse, the weight on the rear-end while going up the range would be far too much for two men. Without further ado we pulled the stove apart and packed the pieces on the stout backs of Blogs and Bluey; they were led very carefully around trees and jutting rocks on the cliff face (cast iron is notoriously brittle) and by sunset our stove had reached home, though not in one piece.

Next morning after the dairy work had been done we started on the job of putting the pieces together. To a layman a stove appears to be as uncomplicated as an empty butter box, but once you get under its cast iron skin and you find undreamed of bits and pieces which deflect the hot draught to remote corners of the oven. The piecing together of our iron jig saw puzzle was not helped by the presence of some Brisbane guests who made many bright but impracticable suggestions. On the day before we had unscrewed the stove and removed the top, the sides had "sprung" back out of line; these sides had been clamped together in the factory with the aid of a big machine cramp, but there was no such vice on Green Mountains which would squeeze them back into position. Things looked blue for a while, then Tom had a brainwave; he went up to the dairy and returned with all the hemp rope we had. This was tightly bound and twitched around the stove; a few kerosene tins of water were then poured over the rope and the resultant shrinkage of the wet rope forced the warped metal into line so that the top could be bolted on.

There was great enthusiasm when the stove was set up in one side of the huge fireplace; we could not help remembering that scene, when almost twenty years later our piano arrived after a very eventful journey. There was, however, one resident of the humpy who resented the coming of a cast iron contraption which smelt of black lead; he was the old cat, Beelzebub – his back and bristles went up and he fled to the big timber; for weeks he deserted his favourite position on the warm hearth stones but finally became reconciled, and when he found the stove to be a good place to sleep under on cold nights there began a partnership which lasted until Beel died.

The experience gained in transporting that first stove proved useful in the following twenty years, during which time six more stoves were packed up.

Beelzebub was very independent and at times as ill-mannered as his namesake, though he was a very loyal friend. For one long period when we were working on a selection over two miles away, Beel followed us to work every day, trotting at our heels like a dog. He helped to eat our lunch and would sleep most of the day in between the buttresses of a tree. After knock off time he led the way home, frisking on ahead like a kitten and stopping to put up his back at every suspicious sound or scent.

One day Tom saw him sparring and cutting capers in the high grass twenty yards above the humpy. Tom went up to see what was going on. A five foot black snake was coming down the hill and Beel, without actually coming to grips was doing his utmost to impede the snake's progress. With a fine mixture of valour and discretion he manoeuvred the reptile around the humpy and steered it towards the creek, then he came back purring. The little job of guarding the humpy was all the more meritorious, because Beel was terrified of snakes and normally ran for his life at the sight of one.

1922 brought an event which was outstanding in our lives, a total solar eclipse. More than five years earlier we had read, in the Queensland Year Book, an announcement of the coming phenomenon, which would not be seen in any of the capital cities of the Commonwealth. The moon shadow was to cut a narrow swathe eighty to one hundred miles wide through Australia and we were among the few favoured people who lived in that narrow path of totality. It was unfortunate that the big city of Brisbane lay just off that track, as three hundred thousand people were, by a narrow margin, deprived of witnessing what even prosaic scientists have described as "Nature's most dramatic spectacle".

It is a strange thing that when an astronomer tells us that a distant star is five hundred light years away, or speaks of the weight and composition of a planet, we are apt to be scoffingly sceptical; yet when he tells us, years ahead, that an eclipse will occur in a certain place, on a certain day, hour and minute, we accept it as we would a railway time table. Much of Dad's knowledge and keenness for natural phenomena must have been sprinkled amongst us, for we all looked forward to 21st September, 1922, as children to Christmas morning. That was the time when the world's foremost astronomers congregated in Australia to test Einstein's newly published Theory of Relativity, but even with that galaxy of great men given in, there was no more enthusiastic group of observers than the O'Reillys of Green Mountains.

A few months before the eclipse there was much consternation in scientific circles, when it was computed that the eclipse would occur two minutes later than the time prophesied many years before. This, however, was not due to an error in early calculation, but to the startling fact that the moon was slowing down in her revolutions round the earth.

The great day came with typical Queensland

heat leavened with a playful west wind which bore the perfume of jungle flowers and the haunting aroma of burning eucalyptus leaves.

Sporadic bush fires sent aloft their columns of smoke like sullen volcanoes here and there in that vast, blue bowl which extends seventy miles west to the Toowoomba Range. Two-thirty p.m. was the zero hour, but as soon as the separating was finished and the poddies fed we set to work smoking bits of broken glass over a burning candle; we knew that ultra violet ray was a potential danger to our eyes even during the period of totality.

For half an hour before the given time we stared aloft through our smoked glass. Our blue cattle dogs, Bet and Bob, became restive, they whined and sat with noses pointed to the sky long before the moon shadow became noticeable. A loud cooee heralded the first little "bite" out of the sun and soon every one had smutty noses from pressing smoked glass too close. For the next hour or so excitement waned, the progress of the moon shadow was exasperatingly slow and we went into the humpy for lunch. It was a strange meal; we were all in a daze, some of us forgot to sugar our tea and some sugared theirs twice, nobody's mind was on food. We took bread and mugs of tea in our hands and went out into the open again; things were getting more interesting by that time. Where sunshine filtered through the leaves of trees there was on the ground beneath, a mosaic pattern of perfect little crescents of light; the little round spots of sunlight had been changed to crescents. The light was becoming wan like a winter's evening, gone was the heat, the west wind blew cold and jackets were buttoned up; the sun, through smoked glass, was a thin crescent like a young moon. Low in the west, the sky was blacker than the blackest tropic storm I have ever seen; the dogs whined pitifully; black cockatoos flew screaming through the gathering gloom; there was a breath of uncanny horror, an unshakeable feeling that The Day of Wrath was at hand. I thought of Pompeii and the lions which lay down and whined in the arena.

With little complaining noises, Mother's orpingtons went to roost in their tree; bells, ceased ringing as the cows bedded down for the "night"; our colony of kookaburras assembled in their favourite mariara tree and the hills echoed with their goodnight laughter. Swiftly – too swiftly for the human mind to record all that was happening – the great drama rushed to its climax. Narrow bands of dancing black shadow raced across us from the west, following each other like Dark Heralds of Doom and behind them, filling half the sky and rushing at us with a speed beyond all earthly things, was a great wall of shadow, more terrible than the blackest of stormy nights. It was so magnificently terrifying that we, well schooled as we were in such matters, had to fight against panic; it seemed a perfect conception of The Day of Judgment.

Swifter than it takes to tell, the darkness enveloped us and then presto! the spectacle of ruthless terror had gone and one of unearthly beauty had taken its place. Where that feeble gleam of sun had flickered out, there was an ebony disc rimmed with green fire and far out into space streamed the incandescent flames of the corona. Even as the beauty of the corona is far beyond earthly things so too the power to describe or conceive its beauty is beyond humans. Outside the growing coronal light, planets and constellations burned clear and white as on a frosty night. Flocks of parrots and currawongs, trapped by the swift descent of "night", fled blindly, screeching and crying like lost souls which could find neither Heaven nor Hell.

Across the great darkened bowl rimmed by the north western ranges, the bush fires blazed into view; snakelike chains of flame many miles long. Far along the northern horizon was a bright golden bar like a summer dawn; from our lofty heights we could see out of the totality belt north towards Gympie, where distant mountains were bathed in tropic sunshine while we were shrouded by black night. The whole colossal spectacle, from the first of the dancing shadows to the end of totality was less than four minutes, but anyone who has experienced a solar eclipse, has lived through a small lifetime in the doing.

I hate to remember the sun's coming out again and its light growing steadily stronger and warmer; it was like sitting in a theatre after the end of a glorious play and watching the stage hands take down the scenery. Perhaps the only part of the anticlimax worth recording had to do with animal reactions. Bet and Bob were obviously relieved but went about sniffing the air in a puzzled manner which was most comical. The orpingtons sat in their bosistoa tree, blinking at each other foolishly until the sun grew quite strong, then some of the old hens went off to their nests with the intention of laying yet another egg. As for the kookaburras, it was the first recorded Australian dawn without their laughter; one by one they flew sheepishly away from their camp tree without so much as a chuckle. We had the laugh that time.

November following the eclipse brought another phenomenon which did not have such happy associations; it was an electric storm. It loomed in the west about two o'clock one afternoon. I was on my way to Kerry with the cream packhorses and Tom who was off to Cainbable to look over the dry cattle, rode with me as far as the turn off. The storm came up black and nasty looking, but no worse in appearance than dozens of others into which we had ridden; there was, however, something uncanny about the thunder; instead of the usual desultory boom of a coming storm there was a continuous sound like an endless procession of great, steel balls rolling down a long, stone corridor. At the cliff top I had a close view of the coming horror and that was enough to send me racing back to Luke's empty humpy for shelter; the clouds were higher than the usual storm and tinged with reddish brown, and as they advanced a constant rain of violet chain lightning fell on the undulating country below.

Swiftly the horses were unpacked and yarded, but before I could get into the humpy a dead tallowwood fifty yards away was struck. I was scarcely inside when there was a sharp crack, my knees doubled up and I went in a heap; the roof had been struck. Very shaky and sick and frightened I got up, pushed out the shutter and looked out; the horses had been knocked down but showed signs of getting up – horses are more sensitive to lightning than men. It was while looking out that I saw something else: two balls of fire were drifting slowly past the humpy about fifteen feet from the ground; they were about the size and shape of a "soccer" football and were a deep glowing red like the coals of a burning ironbark log; they drifted idly this way and that and it was the very uncertainty of their purpose which made them so terrifying. A flash of chain lightning occupies but the merest fraction of a second and if you see it, you know that it has missed you, but there is something indescribably horrible about ball lightning; it can hover about you for a minute, drifting lightly as thistledown yet being potent as a ton of dynamite.

This was but the beginning of a bombardment; for nearly an hour incessant waves of red and violet lightning danced through the cracks of the old humpy to the accompaniment of high-pitched, whining crashes which often overlapped each other like machine gun fire; sometimes my spine would contract and a numbness go through me from induction of some close flash. At times I looked out; the horses were weathering it all right; always there were fireballs drifting; at times they exploded and the red light which flooded the humpy brought with it a wave of heat. Like all good things or bad, the storm passed. Tom had been caught on the high Cainbable ridge; he secured his mare and ran down the eastern side of the spur, where he found dubious shelter under the side of a box log.

He received a bad shaking from shock and at times had felt the suffocating heat of bursting fireballs.

That storm occurred when the planet Mars was closer to the earth than at any other time during my memory, and I have often wondered, if there was any connection. Electric and magnetic storms were common in the eastern states that day, and at night a brilliant display of Aurora Australis was seen from Tasmania.

Perched as we are on the roof of Queensland we have a unique opportunity of studying the weather. We may see, a hundred miles out to sea, a scum of cirrus cloud which marks the western edge of a coming cyclone. We can note during a drought, an isolated thundercloud over Gympie to the north, or Armidale in New South Wales, or perhaps at night remote flickers of lightning which tell of a storm north-west of the Darling Downs, two hundred miles away; the radio report next morning will verify these for us. We can watch the progress of storms across south-east Queensland and know which district is getting rain and which is not.

There are weather signs too which have long been familiar; the wailing of fantail and squaretail cuckoos on a fine morning means a storm. Between New Year and May a flight of screaming yellowtail cockatoos infallibly heralds the coming of rough, wet weather from the south-east. A large, white circle around the moon, usually associated with a mackerel sky means steady rain within two days. An abnormal number of snakes and lizards sunbaking means rough weather to come. There are two unfailing thunder signs in spring and summer. If we wake to find low, dry cloud right up to the door, cloud almost thick enough to cut with a knife, and with it a fresh breeze from the north, it is safe to bet on a storm. The same applies, if in the morning we look to the west and find the valleys and mountains obscured with grey haze up to three thousand feet, while above a bold horizontal line the tops of the peaks appear as clear and blue as on a frosty morning. This latter phenomenon which is known in our vernacular as a "pressure line" sometimes has a spectacular sequel. As the morning heat grows, the haze rises and becomes stratified with transparent layers of atmosphere: these transparent strata are prismatic and cause mirage which distorts the whole of the skyline; the peaks appear to shoot up another thousand feet with flat tops and narrow waists like an hour glass.

When a storm is still a long way off, it is frequently possible to forecast what kind it will be. Our beneficial rainstorms rise slowly and show a high fan of cirrus cloud with an unbroken wall of black nimbus below, occupying the whole western skyline. Should the approaching clouds be higher than the usual formation and rich green in colour, severe hail is indicated. If a storm comes fast along the range tops from the south-west and has a dense, low layer bulging out in front like the dress circle of a theatre, in addition to the ordinary storm mass, we rush to lock our doors and windows; it is almost sure to be accompanied by dangerous wind. As such storms grow nearer, the underlayers of clouds show colours ranging from buff to salmon pink; they writhe and twist in a manner which gives a terrifying preview of the fury of the coming monster. More than once I have been caught by such storms in big timber with a string of horses – they are experiences not easily forgotten.

Storms with dangerous lightning are unobtrusive-looking in the distance, their formation is high, the clouds smooth, even-coloured, greyish black with sometimes a touch of brown, but it is the sound of their thunder which gives warning. Even at a great distance it is possible to identify a type of lightning by the sound of the thunder; it must be obvious that chain lightning which takes the shortest cut from a negative cloud to the positive earth, must make a sound entirely different from that of the harmless brush lightning which writhes across miles of sky and branches out into a hundred leads. More than once when on the point of starting home from the Stockyard Creek depot with packhorses, I have been warned by a distant barrage of separate metallic explosions unaccompanied by any rumble; I would unpack and stay under the little iron roof, while big trees were blown to splinters up along the stony ridges where the homeward track lay. The chances of being hit by lightning are remote, but my job takes me out in more storms in a year than most people experience in a lifetime, so I am not disposed to look for extra trouble. Fatalities do occur; it was in 1921 that our district was horrified when our dear old parish priest, Father Enright, was killed by lightning, while riding near Beaudesert. All who read this will remember the tragic death of the son of Sir Earle Page in similar circumstances. Such fatalities would be more frequent but for the simple fact that people take shelter from storms, whenever possible.

Dad, who spent half a lifetime far away from the

shelter of a roof, had some narrow escapes; there are three I have remembered from his yarns by the fire. The first happened while droving on a treeless plain in western Queensland; a halt had been called for the night near a billabong and the men who were not on watch stood around waiting for the evening meal. A dry storm to which no one had paid particular heed, drifted out of the west; suddenly a bolt of lightning descended in their midst, shattering the camp oven into small pieces; men and horses were knocked down but nobody was seriously hurt. Another time three fat bullocks were killed a bare fifty feet from Dad; he and his horse came to the ground but again no damage was done. On the third occasion Dad and a friend were galloping for the shelter of a bark humpy, when lightning blew a huge, hollow stringybark to pieces by the side of their track; so close were they that they were hurt by the flying fragments.

Those unlucky to be caught out in a severe electric storm are well advised to dismount and get away from a sweating horse, and to keep clear of any ridge with an outcrop of ironstone. On the great treeless plains of the Inland where men and horses and cattle formed the only conspicuous targets for lightning, no drovers of the old school would allow a man who blasphemed or cursed God, to come near their camp during a bad storm.

❧

A little milestone in 1922 was the first visit of our young priest, Father Steele, when, just for one morning, our old humpy became a house of God.

Outside under the tamarinds a chorus of whipbirds, thrushes and golden whistlers mingled with the laughter of the little waterfall. Inside we knelt on the rough slab floor, while the breakfast billycans bubbled on their hooks above the hearth. From the jungle came the call of the lyrebird and closer the protesting voice of a poddy calf in the pen. It was a humble scene and who could help thinking of a humbler scene in a Bethlehem stable.

CHAPTER IX

"May Others Enjoy This Paradise"
– (Our Part)

W E knew that our properties, situated as they were in the exact centre of Lamington National Park, would some day be the hub of very important tourist activities. Green Mountains was not merely a jumping-off point for Australia's most spectacular scenic park, it was the centre, the glowing heart of an area on which Nature had lavished every beauty and luxury of vegetation; an area peopled with those feathered wonders of the world, the lyrebirds, the mound building turkeys, those architects and collectors the bowerbirds, the mouselike atrichornis, the glittering bird of paradise. An area too, which abounded in those living fossils the marsupials, the egg-laying mammals, platypus and echidna, the koala and the flying mice; where volcanic fire and tropic rain had cut fearsome chasms, highlighted by the snowy staircases of countless waterfalls; where the air had the sparkle of champagne and vast blue distances rolled away from the onlookers' feet for hundreds of square miles. We knew what we had a right to expect from such a place when its real owners, the people of Australia, were granted, access to it, but that was something which belonged to the future, when a road would be built.

A National Park differs from ordinary Crown Land in that it is protected for all time against alienation; it is an area held in trust for the people, an area of scientific, scenic and health-giving importance, where the wild life and the vegetation will be kept in perpetuity as they were before the coming of Captain Cook. There were a few people who claimed that our National Park should not be open to the public, that it should remain the happy hunting ground of a mere handful of hardy souls capable of overcoming the extreme difficulties which a visit to this rugged, trackless region entailed. This seemed a very selfish and narrow view; the park, even apart from its immeasurable advantages, represented a tangible asset in public land and timber of some two million pounds. Why should such an enormous asset be reserved for the benefit of a few? Why, since the whole nation owned the park should the vast majority be denied it? Why should those who had the most to gain, the aged people and the ones in delicate health, be debarred from the life-giving air of South Queensland's roof garden, the McPherson Range?

There should be camping areas too, up in the lofty centre of the park, so that families would not be penalised because they could not afford to pay board; so that little, tired, poorer mothers with children – people who need the air most – would have the same chance as monied people. The great park is a national asset and should he treated as such.

It was Tom whose dreams took a more practical turn, who conceived the idea of building a small hostel in the heart of the park, thereby taking the first step in making it available to the people. The preliminary work took years; no money was forthcoming for the employment of outside labour. Some of the near work was done between milkings, but the bulk was done by Tom; for months he camped alone in Stockyard Creek Gorge while making a vehicular road up through the jungle to the very foot of the range; often funds gave out and he went elsewhere to work for wages, saving the money for a further effort. Sometimes he came home to the plateau to help, when the dairy work got beyond us. There were times when a downpour of twenty inches of rain would wipe out a lot of his work, but he would repair it and keep steadily on. When the road was finished, he started to widen the mountain track as much as possible and make it smooth enough for a slide. The jungle track, too, between Luke's clearing and ours was widened and the rocks and roots levered out or cut away.

The track was now complete, but Tom had to find money for the purchase of an engine and gear; many more months elapsed before he was ready. The engine, secondhand, was an old-fashioned oil-driven affair with hot tube ignition and had a large flywheel weighing five hundred-weight. Tom pulled the engine to pieces; the piston and rod, crank shaft and pulley wheel he took up the range on packhorses. The flywheel and engine bed, the latter weighing four and a half hundred-weight, were each mounted on a slide at the foot of the climb. Two harness horses, Diamond and Creamy, which Tom had bought, were yoked tandem. Tom's plan was not to follow the sharp zigzags of the lower part of the track, but to go up the crown of a long steep ridge which lifted from the bed of the gorge in one sharp rise to a point almost half way up the range.

A pulley block was fastened to a tree fifty feet up the ridge, one end of a rope was secured to the first slide and the other was passed through the block; the horses were then hooked on to the end at the block and they pulled down the hill, while the slide travelled up to the tree. The horses were then led back up to the tree and the rope secured to the second slide. First one slide and then the other went up the range fifty feet at a time, and then the block was unfastened and carried up the ridge to another tree. It was slow work and the three-quarters of a mile to the top of the sharp ridge took a couple of days. From there the slides were pulled forward, one at a time, up the graded cliff track to Luke's. At one sharp inward bend in the track we nearly lost flywheel, horses and all. The bend was so sharp that the tandem team pulled slightly across its arc, the slide runner straddled the low stone wall and hung balanced over the drop; Tom held on to the horses while we levered the slide back on to the track. Some years earlier we had lost a packhorse over the edge at that point; he finished up at the foot of the cliff six hundred feet below. The two slides arrived home five days after the start from the gorge.

Now a word about those two stout pioneers

Diamond and Creamy: the latter, now over twenty-five years old, still runs on the plateau paddocks; Diamond has gone on to "horse heaven" some years since. Many people maintain that horses have a paradise separate from man's, but I doubt if any bushman could be happy even in heaven if there were no good horses there.

Difficulties did not end with the arrival of the engine. They had little more than begun: belts, saws and bench gear had to be bought, but how? More delays occurred, then the rainy season came on with more than its usual tenacity. Now came the most serious setback to Tom's work. For some weeks he had been troubled with an abscess in the ear, then it suddenly developed into violent mastoid trouble. It happened at a time when a cyclone and flood had cut us off from the world and days elapsed before he could even start on the slow journey to the doctor. Far too late, there was an operation in Brisbane, and for over a week his life was despaired of. Six months passed before he was able to take an active part in the work again.

At last things took a better turn; there was money enough in hand to make a start; gear was bought and the saw bench rigged up by an expert, Bob. While this was going on Tom and Herb were felling big trees, pine, pungent sassafras and sweet scented rosewood. Ted and his team of splendid horses were hauling them to the little mill site. These logs were rolled up skids to a framework over a freshly dug pit, and sawn through lengthwise, so that they would have flat surfaces to go across the bench to the circular saws. Pit sawing, of which I have had some small experience, is not merely hard work, it is notoriously aggravating: the man underneath in endeavouring to watch his work has his eyes continually filled with sawdust, and there is nothing more conducive to bad temper; two men working out of sight of each other at either end of the saw are frequently at cross purposes, and much effort is lost through lack of cohesion. It is said that in the bush, the most exacting test of friendship is for two men to work all day at pit sawing without having a quarrel.

At last the packhorses plodded up the cliff track with the material to set the wheels going: three circular saws, seventy feet of belting, some four gallon tins of fuel oil, lubricating oil, sixty feet of tramway rails (for wheeling flitches to and from the bench) eight flanged tramway wheels and four axles. We were all set to go, when Bob made a discovery – the holes in the centre of the circular saws were too small to allow them to fit on to their driving spindles. Our mouths took a marked downward curve at the corners; with the transport (or rather the lack of it) at our disposal, it would take a fortnight to get them to Brisbane, re-bored and back on to the job. Bob lost no time on futile curses; even while we were still scratching our heads, he was heating up the little forge with charcoal garnered from a burnt out tallowwood. A worn-out twelve inch file was heated red and re-shaped to the form of a steel bit, then after tedious experimental tempering he succeeded in doing the apparently impossible – he hardened a bit which would bore the case-hardened steel of the saws. So with an ordinary brace, used for the boring of fence posts, and a homemade bit fashioned under the crudest possible conditions, he did a highly exacting engineering job and the wheels began turning that day after all.

What a fine sound the first whine of the saws had and how richly the aroma of freshly cut rosewood blended in with the spiced perfume of the helicas which were blooming in the nearby jungle. The engine boasted of only four and a half horsepower – double that would hardly have been adequate. It was nursed and sworn at and coaxed along, and when it chugged painfully under the strain of a heavy cut, the flitch was pulled back and the engine allowed to get up speed again. That was how all of the cutting was done: first there was a burst of speed by the engine, then its revolutions became slower and slower as the saw ate deeply into the timber. Bob would then pull the flitch back, the engine would gallop again, and so on. Sometimes in thick, hard timber only a foot of progress would be made at a time, a twenty foot cut would mean twenty spells for the engine. It was an undersized and underpowered plant, but hard work and patience yielded fragrant piles of sawn timber, sufficient to form the beginning of the little hostel.

All this time the patient horses were toiling up the range with fresh supplies of fuel, food for the workers, and odd pieces of equipment which were found to be necessary as the job progressed. Over in the jungle, beyond the mill, was the habitat of a lyrebird which had entertained us during the preliminary work, with his calls and mimicry. He was silent for almost a week after the engine noise began to dominate the locality, but one Sunday, when all was quiet, the chugging sound of the engine with a cough and a splutter came from the big timber. For many years afterwards sawmilling sounds were a regular feature of that bird's calls.

The cutting was finished: Bob got his cheque and departed; the timber was stacked in methodical airy piles to season and then a new phase of the work commenced. There had been great difficulties attached to the packing of roofing iron for the small humpies, but the amount then carried was limited, and the greatest length of the sheets only five feet; now we were faced with packing a ton of iron, mainly in nine feet lengths. We made haste slowly, learning as we went. The method which we found most successful was to place four sheets together, roll them until they formed a long cylinder and secure them around the middle with the inevitable fencing wire. A corn sack was then pulled over each end and the sacks hooked by the edges on to the packsaddle, so that the roll of iron would ride horizontally; another roll was hooked to the other side of the saddle and the horse walked between two huge shafts. In the case of nine foot iron, these rolls were longer than the horses; it was impossible for them to see either side or to turn their heads. Only the quietest of horses could be used and only the most patient of drivers could manoeuvre them past the jutting rocks of the cliff and through the miles of narrow jungle track.

Baldy and Diamond brought all of that consignment up; Donna and Creamy, both splendid pack animals, were too temperamental for the job, but they did good work in carrying nails, spikes, bolts, guttering, ridge capping, piping, carpenters' tools and many other items apart from the usual routine of cream and supplies. Glass windows were a source of worry, but they arrived without damage. For subsequent additions to the house we made many casement windows on the spot from our own silky oak – only the glass and putty were packed up.

Things were now sufficiently advanced to get a carpenter. Fred was his name, a bright old fellow with a red face and unfailing good spirits. Never did a carpenter have so many labourers. Fred was the general who directed operations and did the exacting work; no sooner had he cut a bevel than an O'Reilly would swoop upon it, carry it off and nail it up somewhere – sometimes in the wrong place. The house grew like a mushroom and it was a happy job. Fred's good humour was infectious; jokes and banter filled the gaps between the sounds of hammer, saw and plane. And why shouldn't we be happy? Our dream was taking shape at last and with the tourist flow coming our way, things would surely come right – but that was over fifteen years ago.

The new house was perched on the very crest of the range, five hundred feet above the old humpy. It was the spot from which, years before, I had seen my first Queensland mountain sunset and it still remains the most magnificent building site I have ever seen, but it had one drawback – it was five hundred feet above the nearest running water, Moran's Creek. Tanks for rainfall storage had to be erected and the transportation of the material for them was perhaps the hardest of all our pioneering work. The tanks were constructed from sections of curved, heavy gauge galvanized iron; The curve made the packing of this iron an impossibility, so each sheet had to be carried on our backs for five miles. Fred riveted and soldered the sheets together and the tanks were set up on their stands ready for the first thunderstorm.

Then came the great day when we moved up from the old humpy, many packhorse loads of stuff were taken up and scores of things carried by hand. Mother had not come up to look at the house until it was finished; she had lots of fun exploring it. We picked out a little square room for her; it had a large window which looked out over vast blue ranges and it smelt excitingly of rosewood and sassafras and resinous pine.

Once again the only objector to our march of progress was old Beelzebub. He had reached that comfortable settled period of middle age which resents any change, whether it be for better or worse – there are numbers of people like Beel. He was brought up and deposited in the new dining room (it was the first time we had ever had a dining room). We stood around expecting him to be suitably impressed – he was impressed all right: explosive indignation radiated from him after the manner of a retired Colonel of the Indian Army; he swore and spat and fizzed, then put up his back and dashed off down the hill to the humpy. Two subsequent attempts bore similar fruit, so we left him to his own devices for a few days. Then one cold, damp evening when chilly rainwater was running into our new tanks, Tom went down to the humpy. Beelzebub was mewing pitifully; he was lonely and hungry. Tom brought him up to the new "lean-to" kitchen and fed him large quantities of rich Jersey milk – things began to look better straight away – then a rug was spread for him underneath his old cobber, the stove. Beelzebub sniffed the stove, just to make sure of it, and curled up to sleep, grateful for its warmth. From then on he accepted the new order without question.

Packhorse loads of furniture and furnishings for our new house were brought up the range. Even Fairy, the fat round pony, gingerly carried a load of four dining room chairs. Ped, on leave from New Guinea, helped to carry the bathtub, stretcher fashion, from Stockyard Creek. Tables, benches and some chairs were made on the spot, mostly from pit sawn slabs of our own silky oak.

Tom kept the wool clip from his sheep that year; Molly scoured and combed it and Mother made up mattresses and cosy quilts which were stuffed with the wool. Thus, a large saving was effected both in cost and transport, also they proved more comfortable than any bought article.

Our good friends in Brisbane passed around the news of our venture and long before it was built, the whole house was booked up for a coming holiday. Molly gave up her school and came home to look after our new business, to be hostess, housekeeper, "Minister for the Interior" and half a dozen other jobs all in one. She has stuck to them ever since and has been our mainstay through all the difficult years that have gone since that first party of tourists stepped across our doorway.

Molly was also a great asset from the social standpoint: like the rest of us she was mainly self-educated, but for all that, she is the best read and most enlightened bushwoman I have ever met. One could easily imagine her as the librarian of a big public institution; that would have been her true element, but she chose to throw in her lot with us and once having tackled the job she is determined to see it through.

There is something vainglorious about a man's part in pioneering: the cutting down of giant trees, the battle against Nature, where it is hard and real, the defiance of weather at its worst; but a woman's part in pioneering is just as hard – harder still perhaps because of its monotony – and it contains none of the elements of adventure which seem to glorify a man's work. I may say sincerely here that Molly's was the hardest pioneering work of Green Mountains Plateau.

Green Mountains enjoyed a measure of popularity from the outset; the people who had for many years enjoyed the shelter of our humpy were only too glad to recommend us to their friends, and apart from the vast improvement in the accommodation, there were new travelling facilities, which put the plateau within the reach of many more people. Gone was the two-day journey from Brisbane by mixed train, team coach and horseback; the new business made it possible for us to arrange for a car service from Brisbane to within eight miles of the house, and in fine weather the cars actually came to the foot of the climb five miles away.

The irksome tasks of mountain guest house keeping were made far more pleasant by the type of people who formed our clientele; they were in the main the finest and most considerate persons imaginable. This, however, might easily have been expected from people who so loved beauty and nature for their own sake, that they were prepared to put up with any inconvenience and hardship in order to see them at their best. Occasionally – very occasionally – there would arrive some illogical guest who after plodding up some eight miles of sloppy track on horseback, would expect a palatial house with conveniences which were not then available in his own suburb. Others, the unkindest of all, bitterly reproached the O'Reillys for not having a good road to the door, while still others held the family responsible for unpleasant weather.

But happily these cases were rare, and our visitors over twenty-five years, from the early parties in our humpies to those now visiting our established guest house, have been, with few exceptions, an extremely likeable and desirable section of the public. They have contributed greatly to our entertainment and happiness, even as their loyal support has helped towards the success of our venture.

Expansion made it necessary to put on our own service car from the range foot to Beaudesert. This was easy enough in dry weather, but fifteen of the twenty-one miles from Stockyard Creek to Beaudesert were of bottomless black soil and half an inch of rain made them a nightmare to driver and passengers. Bogging was frequent. Added to this hazard were four swift, treacherous crossings of the Albert River which, in sudden storm flood, could cut off a car party fourteen miles from home. Often, too, in the rainy season, the river would stay up for weeks at a time, and all tourists, luggage and goods came and went fourteen miles by horse to the first crossing.

More than once it happened that a sudden cyclone and flood cut us off from civilisation with up to forty guests in the house. Molly was hard put to improvise means of feeding them, while one of us rode many miles around the ridges, skirting the creeks, to return with packhorse loads of bread and meat sodden with rain and flood water.

The chap who went for the provisions, usually I, would perhaps have a day and night in the saddle, in streaming rain and high wind, but all discomfort and hardship and danger would be forgotten in the satisfaction of having triumphed over the elements at their worst – of beating night and rain and flood and cyclone to bring home the badly needed food. The girls at home had the harder part: theirs was the worry and suspense, wondering if the lone rider would get through; would the food hold out; should they ration it; could they get washing dried by the fire so that the guests inside would have snowy linen for their tables and beds.

Many times these problems cropped up, but they were always met and no matter what the extremes of weather might have been, or the difficulties of procuring perishables and vegetables, the quality of the food at the table maintained an even high standard. I would say no establishment of its size in Australia is conducted under such extreme difficulties as ours.

The new business too made the telephone a necessity and here again we had to help ourselves; we had both to build and to maintain it. Fifteen miles of private line had to be constructed to the nearest point of Government wire. Big as this job was, the maintenance of the line has been the greater task. For nine miles our wire runs through virgin jungle and open forest and it is not an uncommon experience during the cyclone season to have four miles of wire on the ground at the one time. Bush fires in spring and early summer also add their large quota to the work. Often during terrific weather, when an urgent call became necessary, some one had to ride for miles along the line to make temporary repairs.

With the pressure of new business it was soon found necessary to extend the house. More big trees began to fall and the saws began to whine again and old Baldy with a new team mate, Blackbird, carried tons more roofing iron up the cliff. Just extend that story over fifteen years and put in new packhorses to take the place of the old ones which died in our service and you have the story of how the tourist industry of Lamington National Park was developed. Year by year the house was extended and the patronage increased and ton by ton, equipment was packed up the range.

To give a better idea of this marathon effort, some figures are set out here based on records which we have kept, of purchases, of cream returns and of guests – a low average weight of luggage being allowed for each person. The estimates are as follows: luggage, approximately 5,000 packhorse loads; cream for butter factory 3,200 loads; wool 100 loads; provisions 4,200 loads; galvanized roofing iron and builders' hardware 200 loads; bed, furniture and furnishings 170 loads; windows, glass and crockery 80 loads; veneer and lining board 38 loads; tools, machinery, engine and lighting fuel 250 loads; live turkeys, fowls and ducks 120 loads; stove, iron, heating, hardware and kitchen utensils 35 loads; piping 10 loads; fencing and telephone wire 70 loads; live pigs 5 loads; miscellaneous, 50 loads. This brings us to a grand total of 13,528 loads or roughly 23,000 hundredweight, transported by packhorses since and including 1913.

The greater part of this vast amount was packed either up the Heartbreaker or up the old cliff track up Stockyard Creek. However for the last four years we have been using the spectacular private mountain road constructed up Cainbable Range by Brisbane Timbers Ltd. The use of this road has reduced our packing distance to four miles, also it has eliminated the use of the old cliff track which was so severe on men and horses.

It will give a better idea of our transport difficulties if I instance the four day Easter Holiday last year (1939). Rose and I had to pack tons of tourist luggage to and from the house not to mention the many hundred-weights of stores and perishable food necessary to keep one hundred and twenty people. The total packing for the four days, amounted to about one hundred and twenty hundred-weight and was done almost entirely in the rain.

The guest house was our sole hope; it was impossible with the primitive transport to make the land fully productive. One by one the big boys who had spent the best years of their manhood in the unequal battle, gave up and left; their youth and the best of their strength had gone, and what mattered more, their hope, had gone. First it was cousin Joe, then Ped and Mick and Herb. They left the mountain and went to where they could make homes and livings for themselves before old age claimed them; to where life would not be an eternal struggle against heavy odds and where there would be at least a measure of security and comfort. Even Tom's health and strength broke under the strain; he went to North Queensland for ten years but is back with us again.

Mother, now in her seventy-eighth year, still spends all but the coldest winter months with us on Green Mountains; she is still hardy enough for the long muddy walk to the end of the road – a walk about which I have heard many young people complain bitterly.

If ever you find Mother when she is not busy – and that is very difficult – she will tell you of her girlhood days in Kanimbla Valley: how, in the days before the coming of the railway, her father used to go to Sydney with his bullock team and bring back his stores and supplies over the Blue Mountains. He usually planned these trips so that he would be accompanied each way on the journey by Mr. Dalton, founder of the well known Orange family. Dalton personally drove his bullock team from Orange to Sydney and back with his stores. She will tell too, of how her Mother made huge casks of butter in the days before separators and butter factories, and how her Father once took a ton of this butter on his waggon up to Mudgee in the gold days, returning many weeks later with his casks full of lovely clear honey from beyond the divide. Once he brought back some pieces of quartz richly studded with gold which a digger had given him. These, she and her brother, Thomas, played with and lost on a little quartz outcrop near the homestead. Many years later when Kanimbla changed hands and her father's run was absorbed into what is now Kanimbla Station, the new owners were greatly excited to find incredibly rich goldbearing quartz on the property – an old chicken had come home to roost.

No daily papers came over the mountains in those days but the stage coaches used to bring the weekly *The Town and Country Journal*. It was Grandfather's habit to read the paper aloud at night while Grandmother baked or sewed, so Mother can tell you a great deal about the Franco-Prussian War which she had heard as current news. She also has a dim recollection of the end of the American Civil War and the death of Lincoln. After the harvest Grandfather used to take his grain to Andrew Brown's mill at Bowenfels and return with his waggon laden with bags of the flour and ground meal.

ॐ

To return to Green Mountains the Stockyard Creek depot was at the head of the gorge before the climb. It was a lonely spot; there was an iron roof without walls and the great tristanias towered one hundred and fifty feet above it. The floor of the gorge was a bare fifty yards wide and on either side the ranges rose steeply to a great height. While working on the telephone I camped there alone for some weeks, and on scores of other occasions, nights of storm and wind, I have taken refuge there, but it was impossible for me to shake off an uncanny feeling which always seemed to manifest itself there. It was not loneliness, that sensation was well known; upwards of a thousand nights of my life have been spent alone under the stars, mostly in jungle. This was something different, a feeling that someone or something was behind you, a feeling which made you want to look over your shoulder, as you sat by the campfire. Other members of the family had noticed it too, something vague and indefinite, but something evil.

No argument is advanced here as to how much we owe to imagination in this matter, or how much to the psychic propensities of Irish ancestry, but Viola, too, has noticed this and she has no Irish blood. It is possible that imagination coloured it; the spot was a dark, evil one; on summer nights, great, black snakes, dimly seen, would slide out of the way of one's horse; it was the favourite haunt of the subtle and terrible death adder, probably the world's deadliest reptile. There were occasional sounds, too, which experienced bushmen could not account for.

It is necessary to reveal all of this in order to give a fuller background to an inexplicable experience which Rose had in Stockyard Creek Gorge. It was a February night; there was a strong south-easter with black rolling clouds and misty rain, a night on which it would be difficult to see one's hand. Rose, who had taken a party of guests to the train in Beaudesert was returning late; she had got into a bog in the black soil flats and it had taken her a long while to get the car out. It was dark before she skidded up the jungle "road" to the depot. Her horses were packed by the light of the headlights, an old trick, and soon her string was moving up the track; with her was a town youth, an excitable, highly-strung chap.

They rode rapidly for some distance up the climb, then reined in to give the horses a blow. It was the youth who saw it first; he had been finding the dark ride a little too eerie for his liking and on looking uneasily over his shoulder saw something.

"What's that light?" he yelled. Rose looked around; fifty yards back, where the track turned a corner, there was a bright orange glow which illuminated the falling rain. As they watched, it came around the corner of the track, a steady flame of light, about two candle power; it advanced for about four seconds, and then disappeared. Rose called out – no answer. The horses suddenly began to plunge and reef at their bits from fright. Rose called again "Hullo, who are you?" no answer. No bushmen ever born would refuse to answer such a cheery call out on the wilds on such a night; Rose was curious, but not alarmed. "I am going back to see about this," she said, heading her horse down the dark track, but the horse reared up, swung around and dashed back to his mate before she could check him. She swung the horse again, but by this time the lad, who had had enough of these goings on, spoke up, "Don't go back down there, or I'll gallop home." This put Rose in an awkward position, a badly scared lad and a fear-maddened horse were a dangerous combination on the cliff track that night; reluctantly she gave up her quest and headed for home with a final defiant yell at the apparition.

❧

There was a sequel, if you may call it such, a week later. I was bringing a big car load of people from Brisbane after business at night, and Rose was driving a string of fourteen horses down the cliff to meet us. The horses, walking single file down the cliff track, were strung out over a hundred yards.

About an hour after dark the cavalcade reached the bend where the light had been seen; here the leader, stolid, unimaginative Blackbird, the pack mare, snorted loudly and stopped. It took twenty minutes of shouting and stone-throwing before Rose got them going again. On more than one occasion afterwards the horses bunched up badly at that same spot; on one occasion in particular, when Viola was driving back a string of horses at night after I had taken a car load of people to Brisbane, she had great difficulty in getting them past this bend. It is most unusual for horses to stop when homeward bound.

We are completely at a loss for a satisfactory explanation. It is easy to say that it must have been a man; these are the arguments against it. Why his silence? – something foreign to a bushman. It was rugged uninhabited country with a one-way track which led only to the O'Reilly's selections; anyone going that way either had business with our cousins or was on his way to the Guest House. The light appeared at less than three feet from the ground – no one on foot could have kept pace with the horses up that steep range. Finally, why the terror of the animals? – horses respect humans but are not terrified of them.

If we exclude human agency what explanation is left? The light was a thousand times stronger than that of a firefly or a glow-worm, nor was it consistent with their behaviour. There was no storm or electricity in the air which would account for such phenomena as ball lightning or St. Elmo's fire. There was no swamp or marshland which might have given off that rare spectacle, Will-o'-

the-Wisp. All natural light is ruled out; it must have been artificial – and yet…

&

In due course I had brought home a wife, Viola. She was from the city, but showed her adaptability within a few months by riding fresh horses, packing packhorses and riding many miles through the jungle alone at night. For our honeymoon we had gone down to Long Swamp Creek and had stayed with my playmates of long ago. We warmed ourselves by the fireplace that grandfather built; we stood within the walls of the old school – its thatch roof long since gone – and we admired the irises which were still struggling and blooming where the garden flourished. The Canadian pine tree, which we had planted to mark the opening of the school, was now head and shoulders above the willows, oaks and gums. Grandfather's great plum tree was snowy with flowers and flame robins were busy amongst the branches.

Our little house was not complete when we arrived home, but we put our mattresses down on the floor amongst the shavings and slept there. Getting our furniture up the range was a task which would take me a dozen chapters to describe. Ours is a funny little house – mostly windows – in among some queer little shrubs, and on the very edge of the jungle. The whole effect was so quaint that we called it Goblin Wood, no other name would do. Our bedroom has six windows, each six feet high, and when open, the thrushes, yellow robins, spinebills and scrub wrens fly straight through, without going to the trouble of flying round the corner of the house. The first winter after our marriage was a severe one on the birds, and apart from feeding our usual flock of thrushes and scrub wrens, we fed twelve wild scrub turkeys at our back door until the warm weather came again; then they went bush. A few of them turned up during subsequent winters – all grown out of recognition.

Later came a baby – a funny, baldheaded little thing with lovely eyes and lovely hands. She was christened Rhelma, but I've always called her Littlefeller. From when she was six weeks old we used to ride up the old Stockyard Creek track and carry her asleep on a pillow in front of us. Once, coming home from Beaudesert, we had trouble with the car; a black night and heavy rain caught us at the foot of the range, and we spent the night there under a few sheets of iron. Our coats and wraps were put round Rhelma, and she slept till morning. Viola and I lay coatless on the wet ground all night. Viola did not complain, but then she never did.

The Littlefeller grew and learned to walk, and I have a pretty mental picture of her soon after she learned to stand by herself, standing in the kitchen door throwing little fistfuls of breadcrumbs to a very greedy thrush.

One day a rifle bird of paradise came to bathe in the top of our tank. We stood a few feet away and watched him for ten minutes, his green and electric-blue shot colours glittering like stainless steel in the sunlight. Though only tiny, Rhelma watched fascinated and made no move or sound to disturb him. Even before she could talk she loved birds and butterflies, and at the age of three could name all the common bird species about the house. Perhaps it would be impossible for the child to grow up in that environment without having her soul steeped in love of Nature. Outside her window at night the ringtailed possums chuckle and scamper in the vines and in wet weather climb under the eaves and camp in the ceiling. At dusk, the little wallabies – Paddy Melons – and bandicoots clip the Kikuyu grass right up to the porch.

At the age of two and a half years Rhelma could ride on her own pony the seven miles up by way of Stockyard Creek arid the old cliff track, a journey which has terrified many an adult. She had lots of busters, but always tried again, and now she is a fine young bushranger, with a special bridle, saddle, riding whip and pony all her own. Only once have I ever seen her annoyed by birds. That was in the summer of 1938 when our poor misguided yellow robins hatched and fed two big greedy square-tailed cuckoos.

Conclusion

IT is not my intention in writing this book, to emphasise the horror or the sadness of the air disaster. Rather, it was to perpetuate the things about it which should not be forgotten – things that will always make us take pride in our manhood; things which give the lie to traducers who tell us our race is degenerating.

Should we forget the Spartan endurance of Proud, the heroic faithfulness of Binstead, the supreme sacrifice of Westray? Should we forget, too, that demonstration of the spirit of mateship and neighbourly help which was brought under the spotlight by the rescue party? Theirs was not a service given under the emotional stress of the moment. It was a re-enactment of the old pioneer shoulder-to-shoulder spirit, without which the Australian bush could never have been conquered. It has been handed down to the sons and the grandsons of the pioneers and is still part of the lives of the men outback.

It is that which makes bushmen neglect their crops and cows to search for some lost child they have never seen. It is the spirit which draws men into a voluntary army to fight their common enemy, bushfire, and which makes them give of their strength and skill to restore the homes of neighbours who were burnt out. It is the urge which makes men plough a neighbour's farm and plant his corn when a sudden operation takes him to hospital. In a simpler way, it is the voice which calls the stranger out of the night to share a Billy of tea.

It was this same spirit of mateship, so splendid and so Australian, that drove bushmen with hearts as big as lions', and hands as gentle as a woman's, to beat the jungle and the torrential rain, and carry two dying men out to safety and life.